Bear Grylls

EPIC EXPEDITIONS

Discover more amazing books in the Bear Grylls series:

Perfect for young adventurers, the *Epic Adventures* series accompanies an exciting range of junior fiction, coloring, and activity books, and a fantastic series of *Survival Skills* handbooks to help them explore the wild. Curious kids can also learn tips and tricks for almost any extreme situation in *Survival Camp*, and explore Earth in *Extreme Planet.*

First American Edition 2019
Kane Miller, A Division of EDC Publishing

Conceived by Bonnier Books UK, in partnership with Bear Grylls Ventures
Produced by Bonnier Books UK, Suite 3.08 The Plaza, 535 King's Road, London SW10 0SZ, UK

For information contact:
Kane Miller, A Division of EDC Publishing
PO Box 470663
Tulsa, OK 74147-0663
www.kanemiller.com
www.edcpub.com
www.usbornebooksandmore.com

Library of Congress Control Number: 2019930463
Printed in Malaysia
2 4 6 8 10 9 7 5 3 1
ISBN: 978-1-61067-939-8

Disclaimer

Bonnier Books UK and Bear Grylls take pride in doing their best to get the facts right in putting together the information in this book, but occasionally something slips past their beady eyes. Therefore, we make no warranties about the accuracy or completeness of the information in the book and to the maximum extent permitted, we disclaim all liability. Wherever possible, we will endeavor to correct any errors of fact at reprint.

Kids — if you want to try any of the activities in this book, please ask your parents first! Parents — all outdoor activities carry some degree of risk and we recommend that anyone participating in these activities be aware of the risks involved and seek professional instruction and guidance. None of the health/medical information in this book is intended as a substitute for professional medical advice; always seek the advice of a qualified practitioner.

Kane Miller
A DIVISION OF EDC PUBLISHING

Bear Grylls

EPIC EXPEDITIONS

CONTENTS

The Northwest Passage

Join Bear Grylls on an epic expedition through the Arctic Sea, as he attempts to travel the infamous Northwest Passage, facing treacherous waters and freezing conditions, to raise money for charity and awareness of global warming.

Amundsen and Scott

Venture into Antarctica, the most remote and unforgiving continent, with Robert Falcon Scott and Roald Amundsen as they travel through freezing and extreme conditions in a race to reach the South Pole.

Bear Grylls

Epic expeditions

We live on a magnificent planet with so much to see. Since I was a child, I have always felt the pull of the wild. I've been lucky enough to have had the opportunity to go on some amazing adventures in some fantastic parts of the world, often to very remote places where only a few human beings have ventured before. On my adventures, I have followed in the footsteps of some epic explorers who led expeditions into the wildest and most remote parts of the world for the first time in history, blazing a trail that future adventurers like me have followed.

When you're going out into the wild, preparation is essential. I will spend months training for big expeditions to make sure I have the essential skills to stay safe.

My expeditions have taken me face-to-face with some of the most magnificent creatures on the planet. Sadly, many of these creatures are now at risk if we do not take steps to protect our planet.

Protecting our planet

While exploring the world is an amazing experience, it is also a great privilege that comes with important responsibility. Human beings are some of the most destructive animals in the world, and are destroying rain forests and endangering animals. If we want to continue going on epic expeditions like the ones in this book, it is vital that we look after our planet, making sure we leave everything as we find it, and respect the natural world as much as possible.

Lewis and Clark

Charting the American West

The Corps of Discovery

When Thomas Jefferson became President of the United States in 1801, US territory extended only as far west as the Mississippi River. Beyond the Mississippi lay an uncharted land, inhabited by hundreds of different Native American tribes. In 1803, however, Jefferson purchased a huge area of land, known as Louisiana, from France. He then decided to send an exploratory party across this territory. The expedition had four aims: to find a trade route to the Pacific Ocean; to protect American interests against land claims made by Spain, France, and England; to make contact with the scattered Native American nations; and to map and find out as much as possible about the new territory. Jefferson chose his personal secretary, Meriwether Lewis, to head the expedition, and Lewis asked his friend, William Clark, to join him.

On May 21, 1804, the Corps of Discovery, headed by Lewis and Clark, set off from St. Charles, Missouri, in their specially designed keelboat.

The western interior of North America was largely unexplored by European colonists before Lewis and Clark's expedition, although Spanish, Russian, and British navigators and fur trappers had earlier surveyed the Pacific coast.

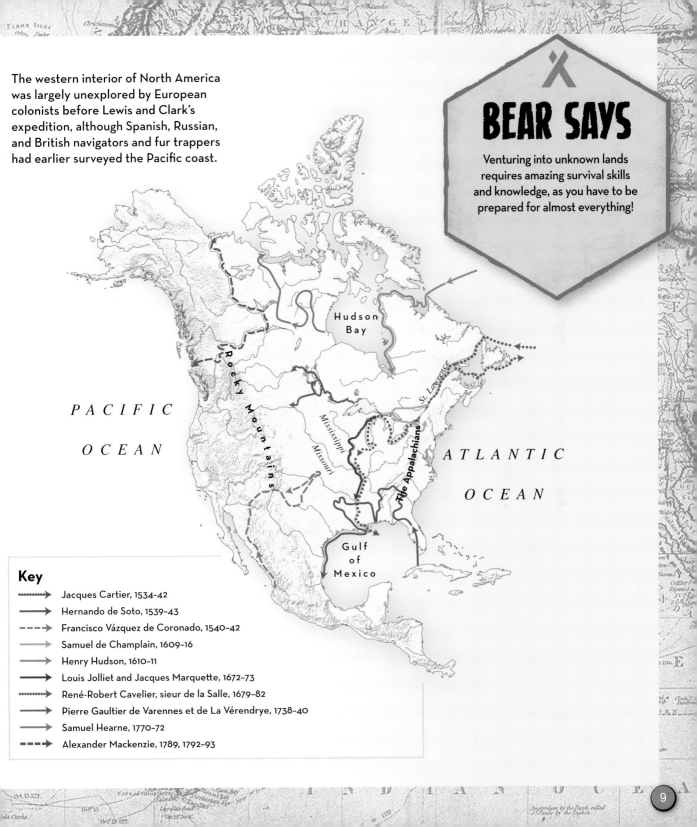

BEAR SAYS

Venturing into unknown lands requires amazing survival skills and knowledge, as you have to be prepared for almost everything!

PACIFIC OCEAN

Hudson Bay

St. Lawrence

Rocky Mountains

Mississippi

Missouri

The Appalachians

ATLANTIC OCEAN

Gulf of Mexico

Key

••••••▶ Jacques Cartier, 1534–42

———▶ Hernando de Soto, 1539–43

- - -▶ Francisco Vázquez de Coronado, 1540–42

———▶ Samuel de Champlain, 1609–16

———▶ Henry Hudson, 1610–11

———▶ Louis Jolliet and Jacques Marquette, 1672–73

••••••▶ René-Robert Cavelier, sieur de la Salle, 1679–82

———▶ Pierre Gaultier de Varennes et de La Vérendrye, 1738–40

———▶ Samuel Hearne, 1770–72

- - -▶ Alexander Mackenzie, 1789, 1792–93

The Louisiana Purchase

When Jefferson bought Louisiana from France in 1803 for $15 million, it doubled the size of the US. There were no roads through this land, and no one was even certain how big it was or what was there. Finding out was part of Lewis and Clark's mission.

EXPEDITION FACT FILE	
Official members of the corps	approx 30
Others who joined at various points	approx 20
Duration of expedition	Two years and four months
Distance traveled	10,624 miles
Deaths	One

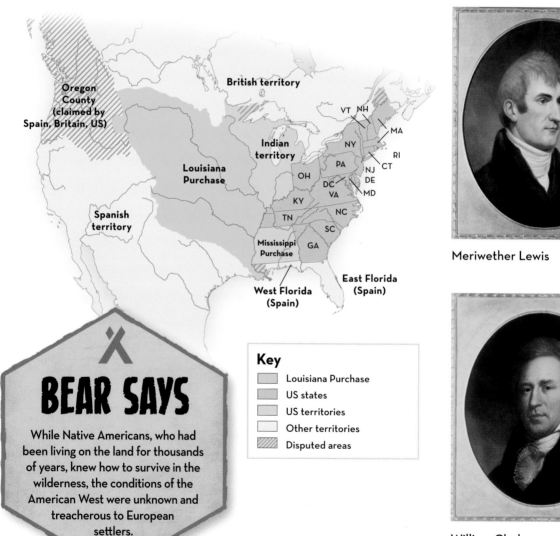

Oregon County (claimed by Spain, Britain, US)

British territory

Indian territory

Louisiana Purchase

Spanish territory

VT NH
MA
NY
PA
RI
CT
OH NJ
DC DE
VA MD
KY
TN NC
SC
Mississippi Purchase GA

West Florida (Spain)

East Florida (Spain)

Meriwether Lewis

William Clark

Key
- Louisiana Purchase
- US states
- US territories
- Other territories
- Disputed areas

BEAR SAYS

While Native Americans, who had been living on the land for thousands of years, knew how to survive in the wilderness, the conditions of the American West were unknown and treacherous to European settlers.

The Corps of Discovery

About 30 men formed the Corps of Discovery, including officers, soldiers, French boatmen, a cook, interpreters, and Clark's African slave, York.

They took a Newfoundland dog named Seaman with them, to help with hunting and guarding camp. Seaman survived the whole trip.

Craft for all conditions

Most of the way would be traveled by river, and the expedition required a variety of boats to cope with the changing conditions. Lewis drew up the designs for the main keelboat, but the Corps would also use, at various times, three pirogues (large, narrow wooden boats), 16 dugout canoes, at least five Native American canoes, and a number of skin boats and log rafts.

Fully equipped

The expedition carried over 12 tons of supplies, including 50 kegs of pork, 30 barrels of flour, 600 pounds of grease, weapons, blankets, medicines, navigational instruments, books, paper and ink, and gifts for Native Americans, such as fishhooks, mirrors, jewelry, and beads. Each man also carried a personal kit, including tools, a knife and ax, and flints and tinder for lighting fires.

The Corps would reach the Rockies in late summer. Even then, it can be chilly, with snowfalls on high peaks.

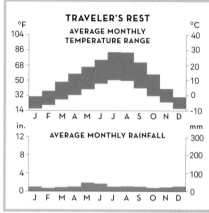

TRAVELER'S REST
AVERAGE MONTHLY TEMPERATURE RANGE

°F
104
86
68
50
32
14
J F M A M J J A S O N D

°C
40
30
20
10
0
-10

AVERAGE MONTHLY RAINFALL

in.
12
8
4
0
J F M A M J J A S O N D

mm
300
200
100
0

KWALHIOQ
LOWER CHINOOK
COWLI
Fort Clatsop KLI
(winter 1805–06) Y
4 CLATSOP
UPPER CHINOOK
TE
Cascade
UM

The men were stunned by the abundance and variety of wildlife in the West, and many of the animals and plants were completely new to them. Altogether, they would discover 122 types of animals and 178 kinds of plants, previously unknown to Europeans.

The west way

Lewis planned to follow the Missouri River north and then west, and hoped to find a river route all the way to the Pacific Ocean, via which the US would then be able to trade with Asia. The Missouri River rises in the Rocky Mountains and plunges down a series of white-water rapids. It is a powerful river and carries huge quantities of water. The currents were strong, and floating logs and branches, unstable banks, and hidden shallows all posed dangers. Even when the men rowed as hard as they could, they managed to travel just a few miles each day.

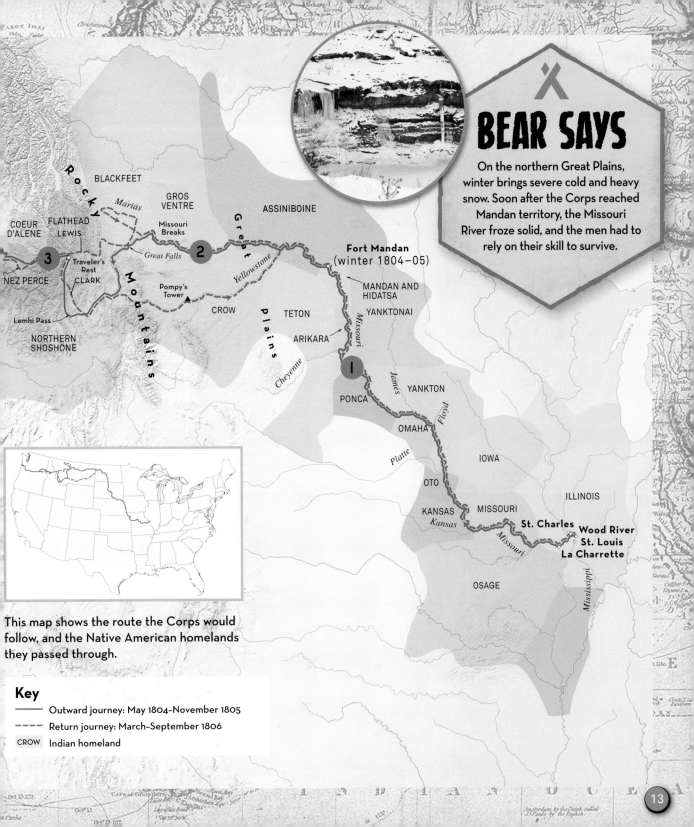

BEAR SAYS

On the northern Great Plains, winter brings severe cold and heavy snow. Soon after the Corps reached Mandan territory, the Missouri River froze solid, and the men had to rely on their skill to survive.

Fort Mandan
(winter 1804–05)

BLACKFEET

GROS VENTRE

ASSINIBOINE

COEUR D'ALENE

FLATHEAD LEWIS

Rocky Mountains

Marias

Missouri Breaks

Great Falls

Traveler's Rest CLARK

NEZ PERCE

Lemhi Pass

NORTHERN SHOSHONE

Great Falls

Great Plains

Yellowstone

Pompy's Tower

CROW

TETON

ARIKARA

Cheyenne

MANDAN AND HIDATSA

YANKTONAI

Missouri

PONCA

James

YANKTON

Floyd

OMAHA

IOWA

Platte

OTO

ILLINOIS

KANSAS

MISSOURI

Kansas

St. Charles

Wood River
St. Louis
La Charrette

Missouri

OSAGE

Mississippi

This map shows the route the Corps would follow, and the Native American homelands they passed through.

Key

— Outward journey: May 1804–November 1805

- - - Return journey: March–September 1806

CROW Indian homeland

13

The Great Plains

The Great Plains lie west of the Mississippi River and east of the Rocky Mountains and are covered with open grassland and prairie. Wind and rain wash large quantities of mud and silt into the lower Missouri River, making river travel difficult.

The Upper Missouri

Along the upper reaches of the Missouri River, the land becomes drier, barer, and more rugged, and steep slopes, loose dry soil, and deep sand border the river. This landscape has changed little since Lewis and Clark first saw it.

The Rocky Mountains

Prior to the expedition, little was known about the Rocky Mountains. Lewis and Clark would be amazed by the steep, lofty peaks, and by the fact that snow remained on them year-round. The mountains in the east were much lower and more rounded.

The Pacific Coast

US ship captain and navigator Robert Gray discovered the mouth of the Columbia River in 1792, while exploring the northern Pacific shoreline. British, French, and Russian traders were also active on the coast, but few had ventured inland from there.

When the river ice broke up in March, the Corps left Fort Mandan. The keelboat was sent back east; six new canoes and two pirogues were taken west. The expedition passed through treeless plains, thick with buffalo, and beneath gigantic cliffs, today known as the Missouri Breaks, which Lewis described as "beautiful in the extreme."

Across the plains

Through the spring, summer, and autumn of 1804, the Corps of Discovery traveled up the Missouri River. While most of the men rowed or pulled the boats, others hunted for deer, duck, and geese. Most days, Lewis walked along the shore with Seaman, his dog, writing observations of animals and birds, and notes that he later used when drawing maps. In August, one of the men, Sergeant Charles Floyd, fell ill and died. He was buried beside the Missouri River, and a nearby stream was named the Floyd River in his honor. The explorers then continued north, through the lands of various Native American peoples, including the Yankton, Arikara, and Teton Sioux. With the weather growing colder, they decided to halt in the territory of the Mandan Indians, and build a fort where they could spend the winter.

Among the Mandan

The Mandan lived in large earth lodges, each housing 20 or more people, and raised crops and hunted buffalo. They were friendly and encouraged the explorers to stay. Their village served as a major marketplace for other Native Americans, as well as French and British traders, so they were used to visitors.

BEAR SAYS

As the expedition moved west, it had increasingly frequent and frightening encounters with grizzly bears, which the men had never seen before. Lewis was chased 80 yards by a bear weighing more than 300 pounds.

At Fort Mandan, Lewis and Clark hired French-Canadian trader Toussaint Charbonneau as a guide, mainly because his then-pregnant wife, Sacagawea, was Shoshone, from the Rocky Mountains, and they knew she would be helpful there. Sacagawea, who gave birth to a son on February 11, 1805, would prove to be an invaluable guide.

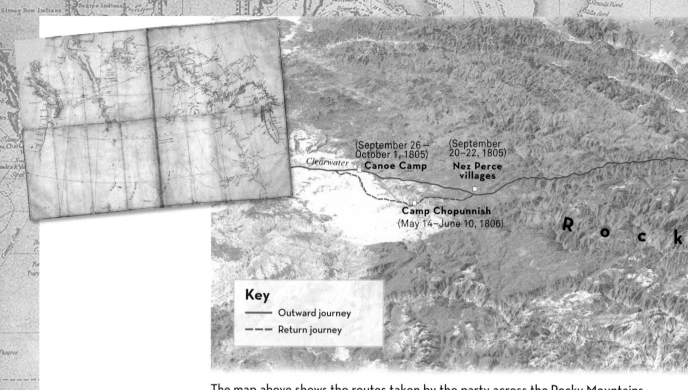

The map above shows the routes taken by the party across the Rocky Mountains.

Over the Rockies

Strong currents and winds made progress slow. The men buried some equipment to use on the way back, which made the boats lighter. But, in mid-June, they encountered a series of huge waterfalls, today known as Great Falls, and violent storms, which together delayed them by nearly a month. They then entered a range of mountains higher than any they had ever seen: the Rocky Mountains. At a place now called the Three Forks, three rivers meet to form the Missouri. They followed the right-hand fork west, but soon realized that they would need horses and local knowledge to get across the mountains. They knew the Shoshone tribe could help, but, frustratingly, they could not find them. Finally, on August 13, Lewis located a Shoshone war party, and with Sacagawea's help, obtained horses and guides, who led the Corps over the rest of the ranges.

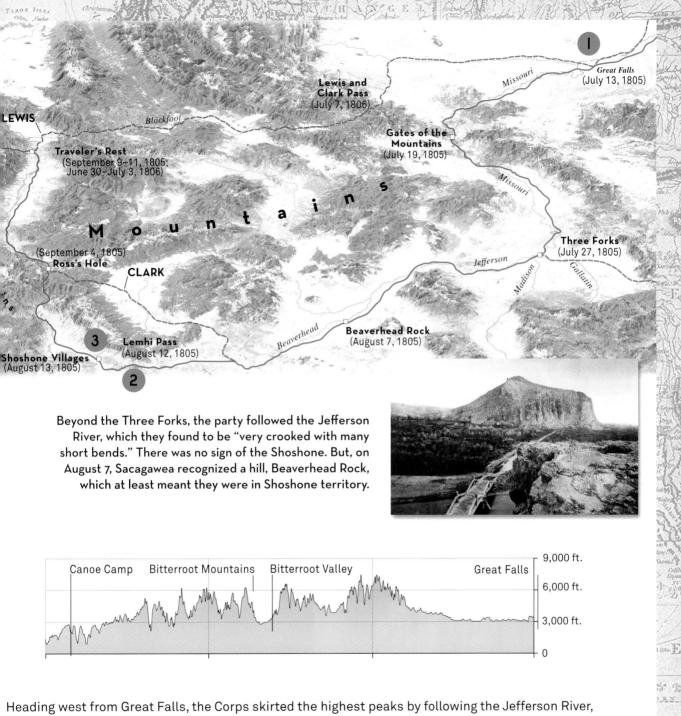

Great Falls (July 13, 1805) ①

Missouri

Lewis and Clark Pass (July 7, 1806)

Blackfoot

LEWIS

Traveler's Rest (September 9–11, 1805; June 30–July 3, 1806)

Gates of the Mountains (July 19, 1805)

Missouri

M o u n t a i n s

Three Forks (July 27, 1805)

(September 4, 1805) **Ross's Hole**

CLARK

Jefferson

Madison

Gallatin

Beaverhead Rock (August 7, 1805)

Beaverhead

③ **Lemhi Pass** (August 12, 1805)

Shoshone Villages (August 13, 1805)

②

Beyond the Three Forks, the party followed the Jefferson River, which they found to be "very crooked with many short bends." There was no sign of the Shoshone. But, on August 7, Sacagawea recognized a hill, Beaverhead Rock, which at least meant they were in Shoshone territory.

Canoe Camp   Bitterroot Mountains   Bitterroot Valley   Great Falls

9,000 ft.
6,000 ft.
3,000 ft.
0

Heading west from Great Falls, the Corps skirted the highest peaks by following the Jefferson River, crossing Lemhi Pass, and then heading north up the Bitterroot Valley. But, from Traveler's Rest, they had to climb over the rugged Bitterroot Mountains.

Great Falls

This series of large waterfalls prevented the Corps from ascending the river by boat; instead they had to portage their boats and more than 2,000 pounds of equipment, food, and stores around the falls.

Lemhi Pass

From Lemhi Pass, Lewis could see that there were "immense ranges of high mountains still to the west of us," and not just one range as his maps had indicated.

3

Long-lost brother

The Shoshone were a nomadic people, traveling from place to place as they hunted and gathered food. When the expedition found them, they were suspicious. But Sacagawea recognized their chief, Cameahwait—it was her brother, whom she'd not seen since she was a child—and the Shoshone then offered help.

4

Bitterroot Mountains

During the arduous 11-day hike over the Bitterroot Mountains from Traveler's Rest, the men and horses nearly starved. Some days, the men woke up in their tents to find themselves covered with a blanket of snow.

Downriver to the sea

Emerging from the Bitterroot Mountains, the explorers met Nez Perce Native Americans, who gave them food, drew them maps, and helped them make new canoes. The Corps then followed the fast-flowing Clearwater, Snake, and Columbia Rivers, portaging when the way was too rocky, lowering their boats down high waterfalls with ropes, and stopping frequently to trade with Native Americans. The scenery changed from barren highlands to lush forests. One day, they realized that the Columbia was rising and falling with the ocean's tides, and that they could hear the sound of waves. Storms and drifting logs pinned them in the river for another five days, but, on November 18, Lewis, scouting ahead, saw the Pacific Ocean for the first time and carved his name on a tree in celebration.

In the Cascade Range, the Columbia has carved a deep gorge with walls that rise up to 4,000 feet above the river.

The river's bounty

Lewis and Clark were amazed by the huge numbers of fish, especially salmon and trout, that the Native Americans caught in the Columbia. One fish, called an eulachon, could be eaten—Lewis said it was "superior to any fish I ever tasted"—but could also be dried, and by attaching a wick to it, used as a candle. Many of the Native Americans who live along the river today still fish in the same way.

The Corps built a fort on the south side of the Columbia River as their home for the winter. They moved in on Christmas Eve, and for the next three months, spent their days hunting, fishing, and repairing their canoes and other equipment. By candlelight, Lewis wrote detailed descriptions of the animals, plants, and people he had seen, while Clark drew maps of the area.

BEAR SAYS

The men eagerly explored the Pacific shore, and as Clark wrote, appeared "much satisfied with their trip, beholding with astonishment the high waves dashing against the rocks."

On the eastern side of the Rockies, Lewis traveled through this valley, now known as Lewis and Clark Pass, on July 17, 1806.

Back from the dead

By the time the men left Fort Clatsop in late March 1806, many people back home had given them up for dead. Glad to get away from the constant rain on the coast, they traveled slowly back up the Columbia. It was too early in the year for salmon fishing, and game was scarce; many Native Americans they met were dying of hunger. In May, they tried to cross the Bitterroot Mountains, but huge snowdrifts made them turn back; a few weeks later, three Native American guides got them through. Lewis and Clark then decided to follow separate routes: Lewis went north to explore the Marias River and Clark followed the Yellowstone. They reunited on August 12 and traveled downstream to St. Louis, to be welcomed by cheering crowds on September 23. They had been gone for nearly two and a half years.

First blood

On July 26, 1806, near the Marias River, Lewis and his men met eight Blackfeet. The Blackfeet were enemies to the Shoshone and the Nez Perce, friends of the Corps. At dawn next day, some of the Blackfeet tried to steal the explorers' horses and guns. One of Lewis's men stabbed a Blackfeet man in the heart, and Lewis shot another in the stomach. It was the only fight with Native Americans during the whole trip.

Clark was here

When the two captains separated, Clark's party included 10 men, Sacagawea, and her 17-month-old son, nicknamed Pompy. Traveling along the Yellowstone River, they passed this rock formation. Clark carved his name on it and called it "Pompy's Tower" in honor of the toddler (though it is now called "Pompeys Pillar"). Later, after their return to St. Louis, Clark paid for Pompy's schooling.

Memorial to Lewis and Clark in Charlottesville, Virginia.

Livingstone and Stanley

Fraught with peril

Into the heart of Africa

By the early 19th century, Europeans had mapped, explored, and begun to colonize the coastline of Africa, but the interior remained mainly unexplored, unmapped… and perilous. Two men did more than others to change this: David Livingstone and Henry Morton Stanley. Livingstone traveled to Africa as a missionary and became the first European to cross the central interior from coast to coast. He befriended African chiefs and campaigned against the slave trade. After he disappeared in 1867, Stanley traveled to Africa to search for him, and later went on to explore vast areas of central Africa himself. The meeting of Livingstone and Stanley, near Lake Tanganyika in 1871, would become one of the most famous encounters in the history of exploration.

David Livingstone

Henry Morton Stanley

BEAR SAYS

In 1844, David Livingstone was attacked by a lion, but was saved by his African friend Mebalwe and a group of tribesmen. Livingstone recovered, but his arm gave him pain for the rest of his life.

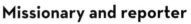

Missionary and reporter

As a poor Scottish boy, Livingstone had to work by day and attend school at night. He trained as a doctor and missionary, and went to work in Africa in 1841. Stanley, an illegitimate child, was educated in a workhouse. He left Britain for America in 1858, fought in the American Civil War, and then became a reporter.

A dangerous place

Most early European exploration of Africa took place in the north of the continent and, even by the mid-19th century, little of the interior had been explored. Central Africa in particular was full of perils—dangerous animals, swamps and dense forests, and deadly diseases such as malaria.

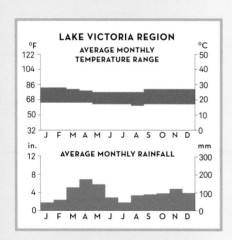

The climate of central Africa is generally hot and wet. European explorers found it exhausting.

Key

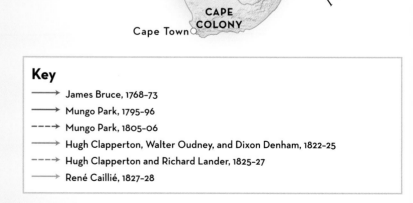

→ James Bruce, 1768–73

→ Mungo Park, 1795–96

---> Mungo Park, 1805–06

→ Hugh Clapperton, Walter Oudney, and Dixon Denham, 1822–25

---> Hugh Clapperton and Richard Lander, 1825–27

→ René Caillié, 1827–28

During his travels in northwestern Africa, Scottish explorer Mungo Park (1771–1806) often became seriously ill. Nevertheless, he compiled detailed descriptions of the region. He drowned on his second expedition, when his canoe was ambushed.

On their guard

The transatlantic slave trade and European settlement had brought great upheaval and conflict to Africa. As a result, the people of the African interior were on their guard when strangers arrived, and quick to defend themselves.

The Nile mystery

The world's second-longest river, the Nile flows from the central African interior north to Egypt. The location of its starting point was a mystery that intrigued Greek and Roman geographers, and inspired early European expeditions to Africa, including that of Scotsman James Bruce in 1768–73.

BEAR SAYS

In 1855, Livingstone became the first European to see Victoria Falls, where the Zambezi River plunges over a cliff into a narrow chasm.

The local people call Victoria Falls *Mosi-oa-Tunya*, "The Smoke That Thunders," but Livingstone renamed the falls after the reigning queen of Britain.

A national hero

In 1841, Livingstone began his missionary work in southern Africa. He married Mary Moffat, and together they traveled north from Cape Town seeking new sites for missions. Together with their children, the Livingstones discovered Lake Ngami, crossed the Kalahari Desert, and located the upper reaches of the Zambezi River. After sending his family back to England, Livingstone crossed Africa from west to east, visiting Victoria Falls on the way.

Returning to Britain in 1856, he was hailed as a national hero. His account of his travels became a best-seller and he gave many lectures. Money was raised to send him back to Africa in 1858 to find a trade route inland via the Zambezi River. This attempt failed. Nevertheless, after Livingstone returned to Britain again in 1864, the Royal Geographical Society and the government gave him money to search for the source of the Nile River.

The slave trade

Traveling deeper into Africa than most other Europeans, Livingstone saw and reported the results of the slave trade: captives being marched in chains, villages emptied of people, and dead bodies lying unburied. He believed that the best way to undermine the slave trade was to develop other, more legitimate forms of commerce with Africa.

Determined and respectful

Livingstone's early success was partly due to the respect with which he treated African people. He studied their languages and cultures, and employed many of them, alongside a small number of Europeans. He carried few arms and was careful not to overreact to aggression. He was also a skilled navigator, as well as being resilient and very determined.

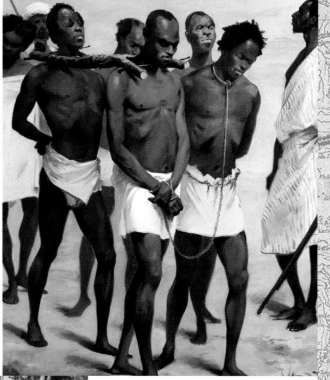

The Zambezi expedition

The aim of the 1858 Zambezi Expedition was to find river routes for British trade, so Livingstone took a steamboat, the *Ma Robert.* However, he found the Zambezi, Shire, and Ruvuma Rivers to be impossible to travel on due to the presence of rapids. Mary came to join her husband in 1861, and he was devastated when she died of a fever the following year. In 1864, the government recalled the expedition and Livingstone made his way back to Britain.

The search for the source of the Nile

By the mid-19th century, finding the source of the Nile River had become the goal of several British explorers, including John Hanning Speke and Richard Burton, and Samuel Baker and his wife, Florence. Speke reached Lake Victoria in 1858 and believed he had found the source, but Burton, part of the same expedition, disagreed. Livingstone had his own ideas and set off to find the source in April 1866, but soon encountered problems and disappeared. Later, in 1875, Henry Morton Stanley would show that Speke had come closest to the truth.

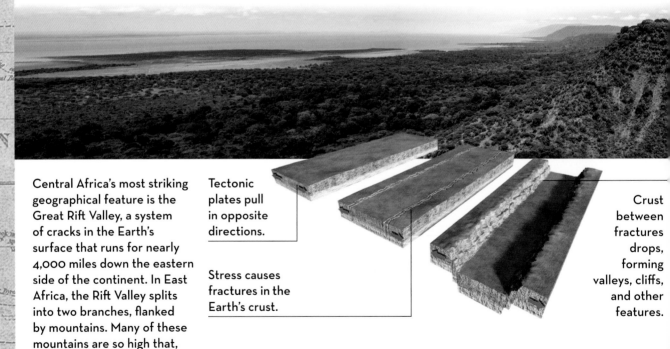

Central Africa's most striking geographical feature is the Great Rift Valley, a system of cracks in the Earth's surface that runs for nearly 4,000 miles down the eastern side of the continent. In East Africa, the Rift Valley splits into two branches, flanked by mountains. Many of these mountains are so high that, although they are near the equator, they have snow on their peaks year-round.

Tectonic plates pull in opposite directions.

Stress causes fractures in the Earth's crust.

Crust between fractures drops, forming valleys, cliffs, and other features.

For millions of years, the two tectonic plates under Africa have been pulling i opposite directions. This has stretched the crust and caused cracks to develop. I turn, the land between the cracks has dropped, forming the Great Rift Valle

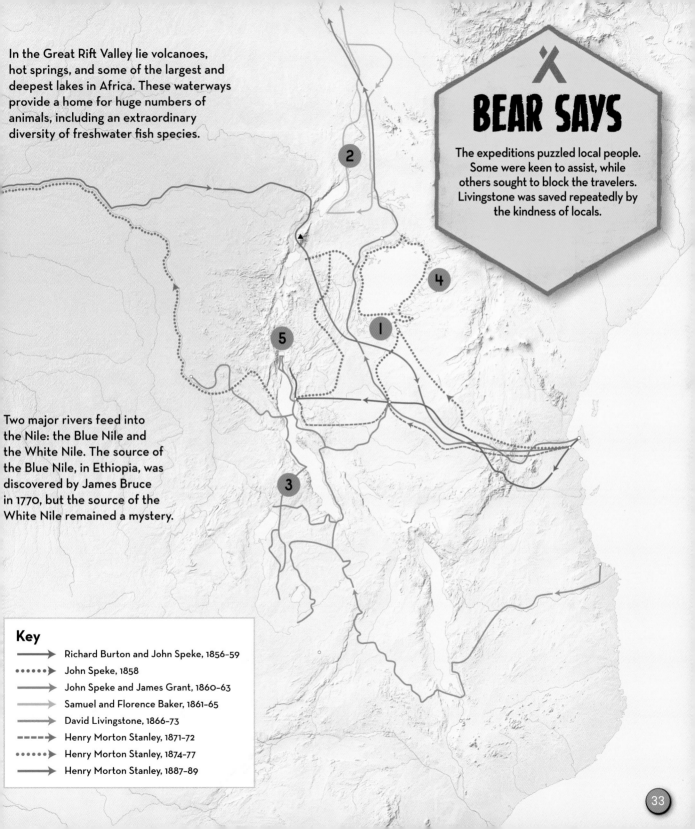

In the Great Rift Valley lie volcanoes, hot springs, and some of the largest and deepest lakes in Africa. These waterways provide a home for huge numbers of animals, including an extraordinary diversity of freshwater fish species.

Two major rivers feed into the Nile: the Blue Nile and the White Nile. The source of the Blue Nile, in Ethiopia, was discovered by James Bruce in 1770, but the source of the White Nile remained a mystery.

BEAR SAYS

The expeditions puzzled local people. Some were keen to assist, while others sought to block the travelers. Livingstone was saved repeatedly by the kindness of locals.

Key

⟶	Richard Burton and John Speke, 1856–59
•••••▶	John Speke, 1858
⟶	John Speke and James Grant, 1860–63
⟶	Samuel and Florence Baker, 1861–65
⟶	David Livingstone, 1866–73
---▶	Henry Morton Stanley, 1871–72
•••••▶	Henry Morton Stanley, 1874–77
⟶	Henry Morton Stanley, 1887–89

Speke's theory

John Hanning Speke and Richard Burton set out in 1856 to explore eastern Africa's lakes and trace the Nile's source. After Burton fell ill, Speke traveled north, discovered and named Lake Victoria in 1858, and declared it to be the source. Burton was furious and rejected the theory. Speke returned to the lake in 1862 and saw the Nile flowing out of it at Ripon Falls. But he died in 1864, with his theory still unproven.

Following the river

Samuel and Florence Baker followed the Nile upstream from Cairo for three years (1861–64). They overcame many obstacles, including illness, difficult terrain, and obstructive local chiefs, to reach Lake Albert and nearby Murchison Falls, a dramatic waterfall in a narrow gorge. But they were still some 300 miles from the river's outlet from Lake Victoria, and could go no farther.

NILE RIVER FACT FILE	
Length	4,160 miles
Width (at widest point)	5 miles
Height above sea level (at source)	8,858 feet at Rwanda's Nyungwe rain forest
Drainage basin of the area of Africa	2,022,286 square miles
Tributaries	White Nile: 2,299 miles long, supplies 15% of the river's water Blue Nile: 994 miles long, supplies 85% of the river's water

Livingstone loses his way

Livingstone returned to Africa in 1866, partly in an attempt to resolve the ongoing dispute between supporters of Speke and those of Burton. He believed the source lay farther south, so he followed the Ruvuma River inland. Soon, his African porters began deserting, his supplies were stolen, and he fell ill. Nevertheless, he forged ahead, and decided, incorrectly, that the Lualaba River was the source.

3

4

Stanley's assessment

Stanley would later locate Livingstone and lead major expeditions across the heart of Africa. During his 1874–77 journey along the Congo River, he traced the northern shore of Lake Victoria and confirmed that the Nile did indeed flow out of the lake at Ripon Falls. He then showed that the Lualaba River did not feed the Nile but the Congo. However, he was unable to determine which rivers supplied Lake Victoria.

The true source

Modern investigations have found that Lake Victoria is supplied by many waterways, mainly feeding into the western side of the lake. Recent expeditions, notably a 2005 South African expedition and a 2006 UK/New Zealand expedition, have traced the source of the Nile to the Rukarara River, which commences its journey deep in the Nyungwe rain forest of modern-day Rwanda.

5

Finding Livingstone

By 1867, when no further news of Livingstone was reaching the outside world, there were calls to mount an expedition to find him. Official search parties were sent out, and in 1869, Gordon Bennett, the owner of *The New York Herald*, ordered Henry Morton Stanley to "Find Livingstone!" In March 1871, Stanley left the East African coast, leading a caravan of about 200 men. He experienced disease, warfare, rebellious porters, and attacks from crocodiles, but finally, in October, he walked into Ujiji, a trading post on the shores of Lake Tanganyika, where he found the missing explorer.

The Royal Geographical Society sent search parties to look for Livingstone (right) in 1868 and 1872. The second party (below) included Livingstone's son, Oswell. They failed to find Livingstone, but brought back news that suggested he was still alive.

Stanley's mission

Stanley warned Gordon Bennett that an expedition would be expensive. "Spend as much as you need to," Bennett told him, "but find Livingstone, whether dead or alive!" Stanley landed in Zanzibar in January 1871. He hired nearly 200 porters and guards, and bought donkeys, horses, boats, tents, guns, and everything else he thought he and his men might need.

The meeting at Ujiji

When Stanley arrived at Ujiji, Livingstone's men came running to tell him that someone was coming. Stanley pushed his way through the crowds of villagers towards the elderly white man. One of his porters carried a large US flag. Stanley could see that the other man was pale and tired, and that his hat and clothes were old and faded. Stanley walked up to the man, took off his own hat, and said, "Dr. Livingstone, I presume?" The two men grasped each other's hands and smiled.

BEAR SAYS

Stanley's first major expedition was extremely challenging and he had to show strong leadership to reach his goals.

Livingstone's last journeys

Though weakened by disease, Livingstone refused to go back to Britain with Stanley; instead, the two men went exploring together. After they parted in March 1872, Livingstone tried to find the source of the Lualaba River. The terrain was difficult, there were heavy rains, the maps were inaccurate, and he became even sicker. On April 30, 1873, he died at a village near Lake Bangweulu. His heart was buried in Africa, but his body was returned to Britain and buried in Westminster Abbey in London. Livingstone's example inspired other explorers and missionaries who would travel to Africa. His reports of the horrors of slavery led to the end of slave trading on the east coast, while his belief that European trade would be beneficial for the continent led to the establishment of British colonies in central Africa.

Livingstone and Stanley traveled together for five months, exploring the shores of Lake Tanganyika.

BEAR SAYS

Biographies of Livingstone remained popular long after his death, and his influence also endured. Two months after he died, the great slave market at Zanzibar was closed forever.

The long road home

After Livingstone died, his followers, led by his servants, James Chuma and Abdullah Susi, decided to send his corpse back to Britain. They preserved the body, using salt and brandy, and wrapped it in cloth. Then they carried it 995 miles to the east coast. The journey took nine months, and 10 men died. At Bagamoyo, the body was placed in a coffin on a ship bound for England.

The Royal Geographical Society presented this special medal to each of the 60 men who had helped carry Livingstone's body across Africa.

Heart of Africa

Livingstone's heart was buried beneath a mupundu tree at the spot where he died. One of his men carved an inscription, "Livingstone, May 4, 1873," and added the names of three of his followers. When the tree decayed, it was chopped down and the inscription was sent to the Royal Geographical Society in London.

Many places in Africa are named for Livingstone, and there are memorials to him all over the world, including this statue next to Victoria Falls.

Stanley's 1874-77 expedition across Africa took him and his party through dangerous, uncharted territory. Of the 225 or so men who set out with Stanley, at least 108 died en route.

BEAR SAYS

Stanley's party spent five months hacking its way through the dense Ituri Forest and repelling attacks from forest tribes.

Coast to coast

Sponsored by two newspapers to resolve questions of African geography, Stanley returned to Africa in 1874. Starting from Zanzibar, he reached Lake Victoria and Ripon Falls, confirming that the White Nile leaves the lake there. Then he made an incredible and dangerous journey along the Lualaba and Congo Rivers to the west coast. His last African expedition, which took place between 1886 and 1890, crossed the continent to rescue Emin Pasha, the governor of Equatoria (then an Egyptian province and now part of northern Uganda and southern Sudan), from an uprising. This trip gave rise to Stanley's best-selling book, *In Darkest Africa*.

CONGO RIVER FACT FILE

Length	2,920 miles
Width (at widest point)	8 miles
Height above sea level at source	5,774 feet in the highlands of northeastern Zambia
Drainage basin	3,390,820 square miles
Rate of flow	134,500 square miles per second

The Mountains of the Moon

The ancient Greeks believed that the Nile had its source in rivers flowing from snowcapped mountains called the Mountains of the Moon. The Rwenzori Range, west of Lake Victoria, which was skirted by Stanley during the Emin Pasha Expedition, was almost certainly the origin of this story. Its highest peak, Mount Stanley (below), is now named after the explorer.

The Emin Pasha relief expedition

In 1886, traveling to assist Emin Pasha, Stanley approached Equatoria via the River Congo and the Ituri Forest—an indirect, dangerous, and difficult route. The huge, heavily armed expedition endured disease, hunger, and warfare, and two-thirds of the men died. Nevertheless, Stanley not only rescued Emin Pasha, but also made a host of significant geographical discoveries along the way.

Huge crowds came to hear Stanley speak about his expeditions, and he received numerous honors and awards. However, some of those who had traveled with him complained that he had used unnecessary violence and that he was a poor leader. His reputation was undermined by these attacks, and when he died in 1904 a request to have his body buried in Westminster Abbey was refused.

Burke and Wills

The Victorian Exploring Expedition

Crossing Australia

Europeans first visited Australia in 1606. After the first settlers arrived in 1788, explorers began to travel inland, but 70 years later no one had yet crossed the interior. The center of the continent remained a mystery, often described as "the ghastly blank." In 1860, the leaders of the newly formed colony of Victoria decided to change that. Gold mines had brought Victoria wealth, and the colonists hoped that a successful exploration of the interior might yield more gold, as well as grazing land, and map a route for a telegraph line that would connect Victoria to Britain. Local scientists and businessmen raised money for an expedition to the north coast, dubbed the Victorian Exploring Expedition, and appointed Robert O'Hara Burke to lead it. When the expedition departed, on August 20, 1860, 15,000 people turned out to see it off.

The expedition was heading into the Australian outback, one of the harshest and most unforgiving landscapes in the world.

Prepared for everything

Burke gathered a huge amount of equipment for the expedition. It weighed 22 tons and included 10 tons of food, as well as tools, saddles, an oak table, 19 revolvers, 10 guns, and six rifles.

EXPEDITION FACT FILE	
Number of expeditioners at start	19
Duration of expedition	16 months
Distance traveled	approx 1,900 miles
Deaths	Seven
Number who completed expedition	One

A colorful, boisterous crowd watched, and a band played as Burke led the expedition out of Royal Park in central Melbourne.

First night

By the end of the first day, three wagons had broken down. The group camped at Essendon, only about 7 miles from the center of Melbourne. The first night was chaos: no one knew where things were packed, or what their responsibilities were, and the camels' presence caused horses to bolt.

The expedition's leader, Robert O'Hara Burke, had been a superintendent of police in Victoria. He was an imposing figure, but he was a poor leader of men, with an impulsive temperament and no experience of exploration. In contrast, William Wills, who would become Burke's second in command, was a level-headed scientist with an inquiring mind.

The ghastly blank

Prior to 1860, Charles Sturt, Thomas Mitchell, and Augustus Gregory had investigated southeastern Australia, and Edward Eyre had explored the southern coastline. Sturt had also tried, but failed, to reach the center of the continent, thought by many to be the site of an inland sea. Ludwig Leichhardt, Edmund Kennedy, and Gregory had trekked across the northern coastal areas. Leichhardt and Kennedy both failed to return.

BEAR SAYS

The expedition was a dramatic sight: 26 camels, 23 horses, six wagons, and 19 men, including four Indian men hired to look after the camels.

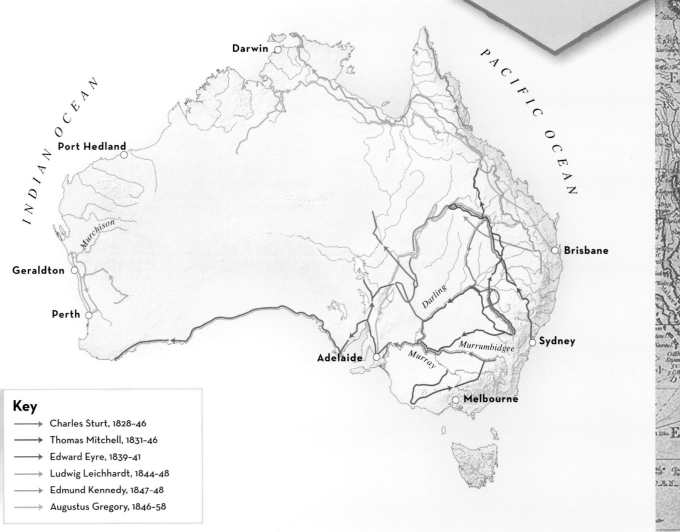

Key

→ Charles Sturt, 1828–46

→ Thomas Mitchell, 1831–46

→ Edward Eyre, 1839–41

→ Ludwig Leichhardt, 1844–48

→ Edmund Kennedy, 1847–48

→ Augustus Gregory, 1846–58

A slow start

In the early stages of the trek, heavy rain and muddy ground slowed the expedition's progress to a rate of just 1 mph. Burke quarreled with George Landells, his second in command, who resigned. Wills took his place. Burke grew concerned about the expedition's costs, and worried that another explorer, John McDouall Stuart, might cross the continent first. At Menindee, the northernmost settlement, Burke dismissed some men, left others behind, and reduced the stores being carried. At Torowoto Swamp, Burke sent William Wright, his third in command, back to Menindee to bring up the remainder of the men and supplies. Meanwhile, Burke and his party moved on to Cooper Creek, arriving there on November 11, 1860.

Cooper Creek was chosen as the site of the expedition's base camp, Depot Camp 65, where supplies would be left for the return journey.

In Menindee, Burke heard that John McDouall Stuart had already reached the center of Australia, on April 22, 1860, before returning to Adelaide. Burke knew Stuart would soon set out again.

Undervalued scientists

Burke's overriding ambition was to be the first to cross Australia from south to north. Scientific investigation was a low priority. When he had to cut back on men and supplies, he ordered the expedition's two scientists, Germans Hermann Beckler and Ludwig Becker, to "give up your scientific investigations to work like the rest of the men," and then left them behind at Menindee. Both men, however, continued recording what they saw, and their observations are greatly valued today.

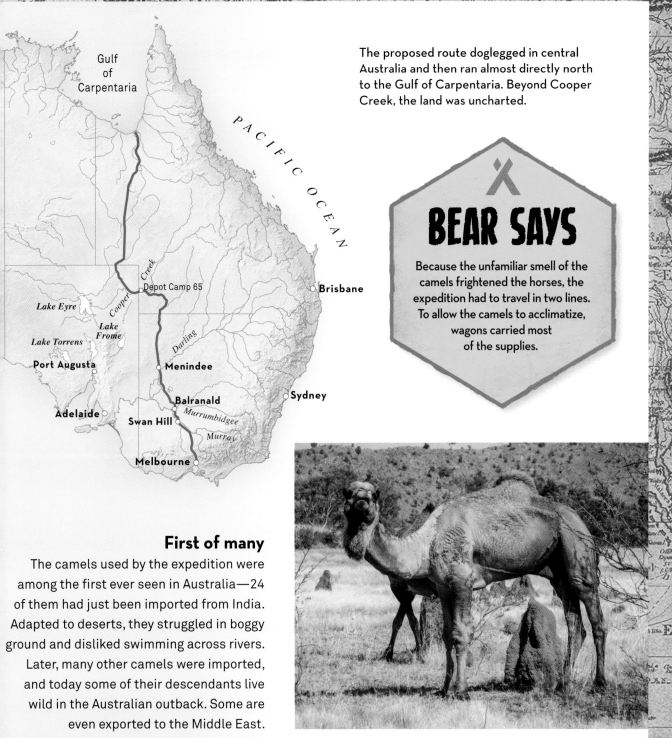

The proposed route doglegged in central Australia and then ran almost directly north to the Gulf of Carpentaria. Beyond Cooper Creek, the land was uncharted.

BEAR SAYS

Because the unfamiliar smell of the camels frightened the horses, the expedition had to travel in two lines. To allow the camels to acclimatize, wagons carried most of the supplies.

First of many

The camels used by the expedition were among the first ever seen in Australia—24 of them had just been imported from India. Adapted to deserts, they struggled in boggy ground and disliked swimming across rivers. Later, many other camels were imported, and today some of their descendants live wild in the Australian outback. Some are even exported to the Middle East.

The dash to the Gulf

Deciding to make a dash to the north coast, Burke and Wills, along with Charles Gray and John King, set off from Cooper Creek. Burke left William Brahe in charge, but he and Wills gave contradictory instructions about how long Brahe should wait for them to return. Amazingly, Burke's party made the trek to the Gulf and back in just over four months, though Gray died en route. On their return however, the survivors found that Brahe and his men had just departed, and were too weak from lack of food and water to follow.

A maze of waterways

A large number of rivers drain into the Gulf of Carpentaria, meandering across the flat plain, now known as the Gulf Country, in great loops, and braiding (splitting into several channels) near the coast. During the wet season, they overflow their banks, flooding huge areas and creating swamps and marshes, and leaving behind many small lakes. These rivers and swamps made navigation difficult, and the explorers were unable to follow a direct route to and from the Gulf. They were constantly wet, and at times the ground was so soft as to be impassable.

Northern Australia has just two seasons: the wet season (November–April) and the dry season (May–October). The four explorers arrived in the north in January, when the weather is very humid and hot, and monsoon rains cause flooding.

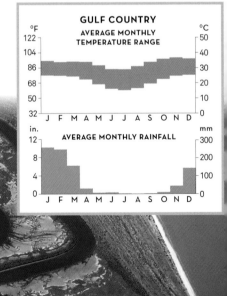

GULF COUNTRY
AVERAGE MONTHLY TEMPERATURE RANGE

°F: 122, 104, 86, 68, 50, 32
°C: 50, 40, 30, 20, 10, 0
J F M A M J J A S O N D

AVERAGE MONTHLY RAINFALL

in.: 12, 8, 4, 0
mm: 300, 200, 100, 0
J F M A M J J A S O N D

Key

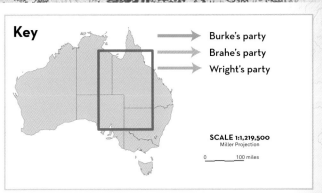

→ Burke's party
→ Brahe's party
→ Wright's party

SCALE 1:1,219,500
Miller Projection

0   100 miles

Picking their way through the swamps toward the Gulf, Burke and his men were apparently unaware of the dangerous saltwater crocodiles, measuring up to 20 feet long, that infest the area.

⑤ Camp 119

February 11, 1861: Burke and Wills halt 14 miles from the sea.

▲ February 9, 1861: The men set up Camp 119 near the junction of the Flinders and Bynoe rivers.

▲ January 27, 1861: The party emerges from the Selwyn Range and descends to the Gulf Country.

④ **Selwyn Range**

▼ March 15, 1861: Three months have elapsed since the departure from Cooper Creek.

▼ March 25, 1861: Burke catches Gray stealing rations.

⑥ **Channel Country**

Long wait on the Darling

Wright's party took up residence at Pamamaroo Creek on the Darling River. Wright was to follow Burke with the remaining men and equipment, but first he needed to send to Melbourne for more horses and provisions. Meanwhile, two messengers and an Aboriginal guide went after Burke, with news of Stuart's progress. The guide returned five weeks later, reporting that the other two were stranded and their horses dead; another four weeks were then spent rescuing them. Finally, three months after Burke left Menindee, Wright and his party set off, but they soon came to a halt as men sickened and died from poor food, lack of water, and heat.

The Exploration Committee's instructions had stated: "Mark your routes as permanently as possible, by ... building cairns, and marking trees." John King was given the task of blazing the party's trail by chipping pieces of bark out of the trunks of trees.

③ ▲ December 25, 1860: The men celebrate Christmas on the Diamantina River.

Sturt Stony Desert

Simpson Desert

② ⑧ ⑦

▼ April 27, 1861: Gray dies. The others spend the day burying him.

▼ April 21, 1861: Burke, Wills, and King arrive back at Cooper Creek.

Coongie Lakes

⑨

▼ April 21, 1861: Wright's party moves to Bulloo Lakes. Brahe and party arrive on April 29.

Lake Eyre

① **Depot Camp 65**

Bulloo Lakes

Mt. Hopeless ▲

Cooper Creek and other rivers of the Channel Country drain into a cluster of salt lakes, which seldom contain any water.

Koorliatto Waterhole

Torowoto Swamp

▼ March 20, 1861: Wright's party halts at Koorliatto Waterhole for three weeks.

Lake Frome

Lake Torrens

Mutawintji

▲ November 5, 1860: Wright arrives at Menindee. His relief party does not depart until January 26, 1861.

Darling

Menindee

Depot Camp 65

Just before Burke left Cooper Creek, he told Brahe to wait three months for his return; however, Wills told him four months. Burke's party took six camels and a horse, provisions for 12 weeks, and guns and ammunition, but no tents. At Depot Camp 65 on the Cooper, Brahe's men built a stockade, then struggled with boredom. After three months, with their provisions running low, Brahe decided that they would wait another five weeks, until April 21, 1861.

Through the Stony Desert

Soon after Burke and his men left Cooper Creek, they entered the Sturt Stony Desert, a large, mainly flat, and very arid area of reddish stones colored by iron in the soil. Some of the terrain is smooth and hard, and quite easy to traverse, but other areas consist of loose stones and rocks, which are very tough on feet.

3

Following the channels

The Channel Country is an area with a huge network of rivers that drain into the salt lakes of the interior. The water usually soaks away or evaporates before reaching the lakes, but when the explorers were in the area the rivers were in full flow, and the men could collect water as they traveled, following the rivers north.

4

Crossing the Selwyn Range

Finding a way through this range of sharp ridges and gorges was a real test of the explorers'—and their camels'—stamina. The camels struggled on the loose stones, and the expedition's pace slowed to only 5–6 miles a day.

BEAR SAYS

Common in central and northern Australia, dingoes form packs of up to 12 animals, but are generally shy around humans.

Blocked by Gulf marshes

The camels could not cope with the boggy ground around the Gulf, so Burke and Wills left them at Camp 119 with King and Gray, and set off into the mangroves with the horse and three days' provisions. On February 11, 1861, they reached a point where the water was salt and the tide visible; however, the dense mangroves forced them to turn back without having seen the sea.

5

6

Delayed by Gray

In early March, Gray, who was suffering from dysentery, began to lag behind. Food was very short, and when Gray helped himself to extra rations, Burke lost his temper and beat him. Gray continued to weaken, dying on April 17. It took the three exhausted men a full day to bury him—a day that meant they missed Brahe and his party at Cooper Creek.

BEAR SAYS

The expedition took almost three months to reach Cooper Creek. Traveling mainly on foot, Burke's party made it from there to the Gulf and back in just over four months.

The home stretch

For the last part of the journey, hungry and weary, Burke, Wills, and King took turns riding the two remaining camels. On the evening of April 21, 1861, with great excitement, they neared the camp they had left four months and five days earlier. They called out as they approached, but there was no reply—the camp was deserted. The men were devastated.

By a whisker

Believing there was by then no chance of Burke's party returning, Brahe and his party left Depot Camp 65 on the morning of April 21 around 10:30 a.m. Burke, Wills, and King arrived that same evening, around 7:30 p.m. The two parties had missed each other by only nine hours, and that evening camped just 14 miles apart.

The Dig Tree

At first, Burke thought that perhaps Brahe had moved his camp, but then Wills saw a blaze on a tree, which included an instruction to dig nearby. They unearthed a note and a box of provisions left by Brahe and realized that they had just missed him. They were so weak that it was impossible for them to go after Brahe and his party. They would have to rest first, then decide what to do.

Survival in the outback

From Menindee northward, the expedition traveled through the unmapped and perilous Australian outback. This desert area receives less than 10 inches of rain a year; in summer, temperatures may reach 122°F and rivers and water holes shrink or disappear. Burke had been warned not to travel through the outback in summer, but he was so determined to beat Stuart that he ignored that advice. Staying alive in the outback requires the right equipment and knowledge—which the explorers did not have. In contrast, the continent's Aboriginal peoples, who had lived in the Australian interior for thousands of years, had strategies and skills to help them survive. Although they were wary of the Europeans and their horses and camels, and sometimes hostile, they often helped the explorers find water and food.

The outback is a beautiful but arid land, with very little food and water.

Searing heat

At Cooper Creek, Wills recorded afternoon shade temperatures of between 100–109°F. To replace the liquid they sweated in such conditions, the explorers needed to drink about 15 liters of water a day, but they only carried about 3 liters each a day.

Water loss (%)

8

6

4

2

0

| Body less able to control temperature | Loss of stamina | Loss of muscle power; heat cramps | Heatstroke, coma, death |

When water loss from the body reaches just six percent, coma and death can follow quickly.

Attuned to an arid land

The Aborigines were hunter-gatherers, skilled at desert living. They knew where to dig for water, how to follow animal tracks to a water hole, and which plants held moisture. They could also find, prepare, and eat a variety of plants and animals.

When gathering foods, Aborigines often placed them in vessels like these, known as coolamons.

Water holes were vital sources of water for Aborigines. The explorers failed to appreciate their usefulness and their spiritual significance for the Aborigines.

A widespread arid-country plant with a distinctive flower, Sturt's desert pea sheds seeds that lie dormant until the next rainfall, then sprout quickly.

Waiting for rain

Desert plants and animals have adapted to arid conditions. Some animals burrow underground or sleep during the day and are active at night, when it is cooler. Plants with long roots can reach water deep underground. Some have seeds that remain inactive until rain comes, at which point the plant flowers, produces new seeds, and dies within a few days.

BEAR SAYS

To avoid extreme heat, water-holding frogs estivate (lie dormant) underground for long spells, only emerging after it rains to feed and breed.

Attempting to reach Mount Hopeless, Burke, Wills, and King became lost in desert country.

Missed again

Having missed Brahe, Burke decided to follow the Cooper and Strzelecki creeks to a police outpost at Mount Hopeless, 150 miles away. King reburied Brahe's box under the Dig Tree to prevent Aborigines finding it, but Burke decided to leave no message. Soon the camels died, and the men became stranded on the Cooper, about 20 miles from Depot Camp 65. Meanwhile, Brahe met Wright and his party, and the two men returned to the depot. Finding no evidence of Burke's return, they left no sign of their visit. By then, Burke, Wills, and King were in dire straits, only just surviving on a plant called nardoo and help from Aborigines. Wills struggled back to the depot and buried their journals under the Dig Tree. Soon after his return, he and Burke died.

Going native

Aborigines made food from the spores of the nardoo plant, a type of fern. Nardoo contains a chemical called thiaminase, which causes vitamin B_1 deficiency and can impair digestion and lead to weakness. The Aborigines washed and roasted the nardoo before grinding it, which destroyed the thiaminase. The explorers did not, and this probably contributed to the deaths of Burke and Wills.

BEAR SAYS

Nardoo was processed using flat grinding stones known as nardoo stones, which the Aborigines left at the edges of watercourses.

The Aborigines would not have taught Burke and Wills how to prepare nardoo, as the preparation was generally women's work and would not have been shown to guests such as the European explorers.

Lost leader

Wills became so feeble that Burke and King went to seek help from the local Aborigines. When Burke grew too weak to stand, he asked King to leave him alone with his pistol. Part of his last letter read, "King has behaved nobly and ... has stayed with me till the last."

At their camp at Bulloo Lakes, Wright and his men were beset by disease and plagues of rats. Among the sick was Ludwig Becker, who nevertheless continued to keep records even when he could barely sit up. He died on April 29, 1861.

The death of Wills

King went back to Wills and found that he too had died, and his body had been covered with branches by Aborigines. King was now alone. He took a letter Wills had left for his father, which began, "These are probably the last lines you will ever get from me. We are on the point of starvation." It ended, "Spirits are excellent."

Bearer of bad news

By the time Burke and Wills died, Brahe's and Wright's parties had struggled back to Menindee. Brahe then rode on to Melbourne, bearing news of the expedition's failure.

1861	APRIL	MAY	JUNE
Burke, Wills & party	23rd—Leave Cooper Creek for Mount Hopeless	7th—Last camel dies, stranded 23rd—Wills returns to Cooper Creek	28th—Approximate date of the deaths of Burke & Wills
Brahe & party		8th—Brahe returns to Cooper Creek with Wright, but they find no sign of Burke's party	18th—Arrive back at Menindee
Wright & party	29th—Death of Becker	8th—Wright returns to Cooper Creek with Brahe	18th—Arrive back at Menindee

Burke laid to rest
After finding King, Howitt located the bodies of Burke and Wills and buried them near where they died. He wrapped Burke's body in a British flag.

Rescue and remembrance

By June 1861, there had been no news in Melbourne from any of the explorers for six months, and public concern began to mount. Too late, the Victorian Exploration Committee and the governments of South Australia and Queensland sent out rescue expeditions. The Victorian party, led by Alfred Howitt, found King and sent news that Burke and Wills were dead. Howitt later brought their bodies home for a huge state funeral in Melbourne, and the two men were mourned as tragic heroes. Nevertheless, there was an investigation of what had gone wrong, and Burke, Brahe, and Wright were all criticized for their actions. The expedition had, however, filled out the map of the Australian interior, proving that there was no inland sea, and the rescue expeditions expanded that knowledge even further.

Alfred Howitt's expedition reached the Dig Tree in September 1861 and found John King. Meanwhile, other relief expeditions traveled to the gulf, and search parties set out from Queensland and South Australia. These expeditions contributed greatly to knowledge of the interior.

Sole survivor

King had surviv4ed with the help of the Aborigines, but he was so ill when rescued that Howitt thought he might not survive. Although he grew stronger after a few days, he was mentally and physically damaged by his ordeal, and was not keen to talk about his exploits when he returned to Melbourne, despite being greeted as a hero. He never fully recovered his health, and died at age 33.

State funeral

A public burial and memorial were planned for Burke and Wills. Howitt brought the men's bones back to Melbourne, and on January 21, 1863, Victoria held its first state funeral; 60,000 people watched the procession, which was headed by a huge funeral car.

Stuart's success

John McDouall Stuart and his party had begun their attempt at the south-north crossing on January 1, 1861, but due to heat, lack of water, and hostile Aborigines, returned to Adelaide. They set off again in October, made it to the north coast in July 1862, and returned to Adelaide in triumph—on the day of Burke and Wills' funeral.

Bear Grylls

The Northwest Passage

There are still some places in the world where few people—if any—have ventured. Back in 2010, one such location beckoned to me: the infamous Northwest Passage, a route through the Arctic Ocean connecting the Atlantic to the Pacific. In the past, many attempted to navigate this fabled trading route. It's an unforgiving landscape of freezing temperatures, high seas, sea ice, polar bears, and weather that can turn without warning. Perhaps most famous was Sir John Franklin's expedition in 1845. Franklin was prepared with two boats outfitted with steamer engines: HMS *Erebus* and HMS *Terror*. The expedition never made it. The boats and crew were lost. Yet six of us were planning to attempt it in a tiny Zodiac Rigid Inflatable Boat (RIB). A small team and I were heading out with the aim of both raising awareness of global warming and raising money for a wonderful children's charity called Global Angels. But no matter how prepared we were, we had no idea just what we were letting ourselves in for.

Our Zodiac Rib

Our 36-foot Shockwave Zodiac RIB, powered by three 300-horsepower Mercury Verado Outboard engines. The aluminum hull was designed to be lightweight and tough.

The Beaufort Sea

Departing on August 30, 2010, we would cross 1,700 nautical miles of treacherous Arctic Ocean. We started on Canada's Baffin Island—the fifth-biggest island in the world—and wove through the archipelago, a wild mass of islands that are usually connected by thick ice. From there, we traversed into the Beaufort Sea, named after Sir Francis Beaufort, who developed the Beaufort wind force scale—and we faced mighty winds here! Weather was a constant threat: driving rains, frigid winds, and thick mists often slowed our progress to a crawl. Even 74° above the Equator, the landscape is rich with bird life, seals, and whales.

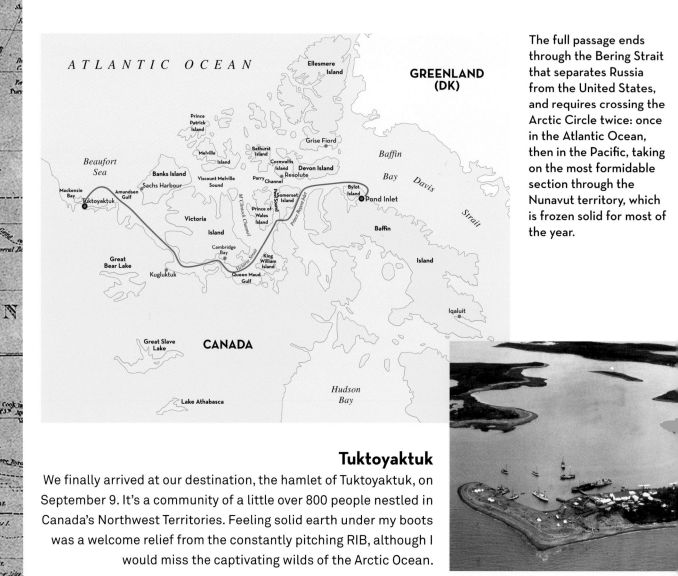

The full passage ends through the Bering Strait that separates Russia from the United States, and requires crossing the Arctic Circle twice: once in the Atlantic Ocean, then in the Pacific, taking on the most formidable section through the Nunavut territory, which is frozen solid for most of the year.

Tuktoyaktuk

We finally arrived at our destination, the hamlet of Tuktoyaktuk, on September 9. It's a community of a little over 800 people nestled in Canada's Northwest Territories. Feeling solid earth under my boots was a welcome relief from the constantly pitching RIB, although I would miss the captivating wilds of the Arctic Ocean.

Sir J. Franklin

Sir John Franklin

In 1845, British Royal Naval Officer Rear Admiral Sir John Franklin was tasked to chart the remaining 300 miles of the Arctic coastline left after his first successful voyage. He prepared two sailing ships—HMS *Erebus* and HMS *Terror*—outfitted with new steam engines. The expedition never made it. All hands perished.

Sir John Franklin

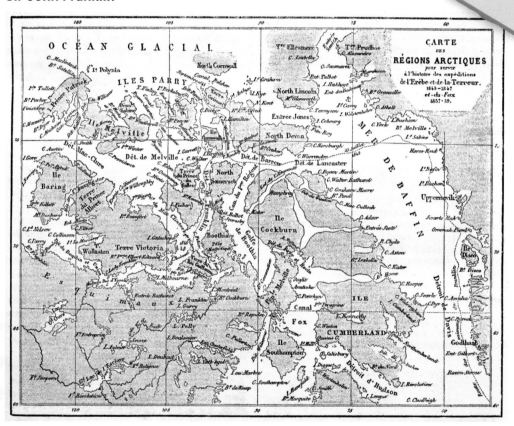

The fate of the crew

It was three years before a rescue mission was sent. They found nothing. Nine years later, Inuit hunters told explorer Dr. John Rae that the expedition had become icebound. The men had abandoned their vessels but succumbed to disease, hypothermia, and starvation. Some had even resorted to cannibalism. Rae failed to find any signs of Sir Franklin's body.

Danger Ahoy!

Magical desolation

As we prepared for the expedition, thoughts of what could go wrong kept me awake at night. The remoteness of the Northwest Passage is striking. Ferocious winds create big seas that were more than capable of smashing up a boat like ours, and the chance of becoming trapped in frozen sea ice was at times very high. The thought of the dangers ahead often feels intimidating, yet the moment the sun rises over the ocean you can't help but be captivated by the magical desolation.

The Northwest Passage
Although barren, there is something magical about this landscape.

Flotsam

An additional unexpected threat on the water came from the flotsam (debris) that washed out from the mighty rivers. Sometimes huge tree trunks were swept out to sea, which along with the sea ice made a terrifying natural obstacle course. Even in calm seas, we often had to strap ourselves in. If we struck anything, we would be hurled out of our seats and into the frozen water.

BEAR SAYS

At -28°F, if you fall in the Arctic water—even in your dry suit—you won't live longer than 15 minutes ... if you're lucky!

Lethal temperatures

To increase our chances of success, we set out in the summer months, when average temperatures range from 14–50°F. In the winter, it can sink to -28°F. When the wind kicks in, expect those temperatures to plummet further. Then factor in wind chill from winds blowing between 12–180 mph.

Big seas

The weather changes almost instantly. One moment we're cruising over calm water, then the sky darkens, winds pick up, and the waves rise. These big seas relentlessly pummeled our tiny craft. One rogue wave jolted one of our team clean off his seat, whacking his head and drawing a lot of blood.

Rough Arctic seas

Waves of up to 16 feet have been recorded in regions where the sea is supposed to be frozen solid.

Sea ice

Sea ice was by far our biggest threat. Past expeditions were forced to cut their way through thick ice, but due to global warming, we could navigate around it. Sometimes though, we had no choice but to push through the ice. If our boat struck one of these monstrous pieces of floating ice, it would potentially prove devastating to the expedition.

Our Zodiac RIB plowing through the ocean
Due to global warming, our little boat enabled us to explore areas where nobody had been able to venture before.

Sea ice
Sea ice was a constant threat, against which we had no protection.

Keeping a lookout
We remained vigilant. Picking our way through the ice felt like playing a giant game of checkers ... and one false move could be disastrous.

BEAR SAYS

Sea ice is frozen ocean water, whereas icebergs and glaciers are formed on land, before breaking off and floating out to sea.

The big melt

In the deepest winter, the ice sheets extend across the region in an unbroken mass, reaching up to 13 feet thick. Only recently has the ice melted away in the summer months with such severity to make our journey possible. The open water before us was a clear sign that global warming is affecting this region at an alarming rate.

The unseen threat

Danger didn't just come from the ice we could see above the water; the rest of the ice floated just beneath the surface, extensive and shallow enough to destroy our hull. It was almost impossible to see, especially against the white frothing of the waves, and it made us feel very vulnerable.

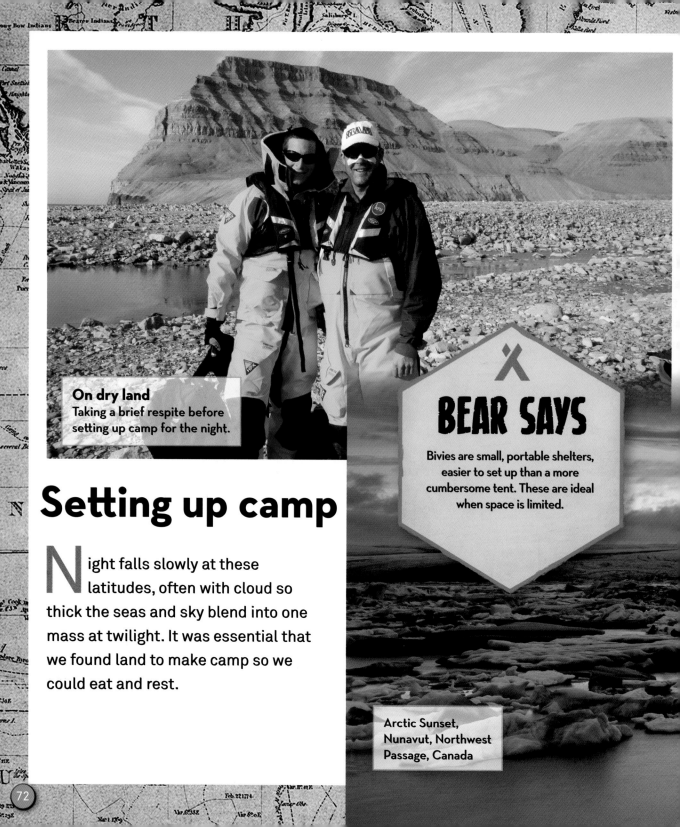

On dry land
Taking a brief respite before setting up camp for the night.

Setting up camp

Night falls slowly at these latitudes, often with cloud so thick the seas and sky blend into one mass at twilight. It was essential that we found land to make camp so we could eat and rest.

BEAR SAYS

Bivies are small, portable shelters, easier to set up than a more cumbersome tent. These are ideal when space is limited.

Arctic Sunset, Nunavut, Northwest Passage, Canada

Camp routine

The first task was to make a fire to warm our cold bodies. With temperatures sliding, it was a task we always aimed to achieve quickly. We gathered fuel from driftwood to make a bonfire. Camp food was simple boil-in-the-bag rations, then we'd hunker down in our bivies for a welcome sleep.

Campfire
Keeping the campfire going was important; we burned whatever fuel we could find.

lose encounters

aking sure our RIB was securely anchored to the island was essential. One fear we all shared was waking find our boat had drifted away in the night, leaving us stranded. We'd take shifts on boat watch, which so doubled as a bear watch. The scent of our food could carry for miles, and the last thing we needed as a close encounter with a hungry polar bear! We kept a shotgun and a can of bear spray handy at all times.

Grave encounter

On a barren island, no more than 600 feet in diameter, we encountered something very unexpected when we set up camp: multiple graves. Little more than stones delineating the outline of a body, they strongly resembled western graves in style—not Inuit. Closer inspection revealed human bones, empty bullet cartridges, and fragments of fabric. Could this be the remains of Sir Franklin himself?

Hungry

Immediately, our thoughts went back to tales of Sir Franklin's expedition. How many years had they lived on this inhospitable lump of rock? What would that do to the mind? And, as we tucked into our boil-in-the-bag rations, how long had they endured before resorting to cannibalism?

BEAR SAYS

We suspected that this burial was not an Inuit one. We had stumbled over what we thought could be the remains of the Franklin expedition.

Shipwrecked

As night fell, we were driven by curiosity. We explored the rest of this tiny island by the light of the moon and our flashlights. It didn't take very long. The first discovery was what looked like the remains of a wooden mast half buried in the shallow mud. That, together with the graves, made me wonder—had they run aground in the foul darkness or been trapped in the ice, unable to move?

An unexpected find

Hurrying back to camp, one of our team accidentally kicked what he thought was a rock—but the hollow clattering sound soon revealed the macabre truth: it was a human skull! Who was this poor man? Was he the last member of the team, left to bury his companions or turn to cannibalism, before dying alone? It was a chilling thought to go to sleep with.

BEAR SAYS

The cannibalistic tribes of Polynesia called human flesh "long pig," due to the look of it, rather than the taste.

Refueling

Whenever we stopped for rest or fuel, it took a long time to get our "land legs" back!

No matter how reliable our trusty Zodiac RIB was proving to be, those three outboard motors needed fueling. We were fortunate that the Inuit living across Nunavut supplied us with regular gasoline stops. Using battered pickup trucks they helped transport small barrels of fuel to the most seemingly inaccessible of beaches.

Repairs on the go

Mother Nature doesn't care how good your gear is; she'll pummel it to destruction every chance she gets. Our hull took a pounding, and the engines were damaged by small lumps of sea ice, forcing us to improvise repairs with whatever we had at hand. While such problems can often wear people's spirits down, they are the essence of adventure: solve one problem, then move on to the next. Little by little, you'll reach your destination.

Local knowledge

The Inuit are a gracious people, always offering us gifts, well-wishes, and warnings of the dangers ahead. Their knowledge is based on firsthand experience and wisdom passed down for the last 4,000 years. Wherever you are in the world, advice like this is like gold dust, and often comes wrapped in tales from folklore.

ᑕᐅᑐᒃᑲᐅᔭᕐᓂᒃ

ᐃᓄᑦ ᔪᐊᕝ ᐃᓇᕘᖓᓂᒃ ᓄᒪᐅᒥᑕ ᑐᑐᓐᑕᐊᖅᖁᐸᕐᒪᕗᐊᖓᓐᒃ. ᓇᓇᐊᒃᑐᓄ
ᔪᕐᔪᐊᕙᕐᓕᓇ ᖔᖁᑐᓄ, ᓇᐅᕐᕮᒃᑲᑦᐸᒃᒥᓐ ᐱᕈᐅᒻᒃ ᐸᕰᒍᐱᕐᓄᕐᐊᕤᒃᑦ
ᑕᕐᓇᒻᔪᓐ ᑕᒪᓄᓂᔪᕐᔴᒃ. ᓇᐅᕮᐊᕐ ᖅᕮᓐᒃᒧᒃᖁᕤᐅᖓᔪᓄᒻᖤ, ᔪᒪᓂᕮᖁᖁᔪᖓᕤ,
ᔪᔪᓄᐊᓐᓕᐱᒻᕮᓐᖁᖔᕤ ᓄᓇᒻᒄᓐᒄ. ᕮᔴᒻ ᑲᕐᖤᕮᑲᕐᐦᒻᕤᒻᒃᔾᖑᒻ,
ᓇᐅᕮᓄ ᑕᐸᓂᒪᕮᐃᑲᕐᒄᓄᕐᒃᖔᕮᕮᒻᕤᖅᒄ. ᓇᒫᒻᒃᔪᒻ ᔪᕤᕮᒄ ᐃᓕᓄᕮ ᕮᒄᓇᕐᒄᒄᖓᖓ.
ᕮᔴᒻ ᔪᒃᔴᔪᑕᐸᕐᕤᕮᖑᖤᕤ ᐃᖔᕰᐦᖁᕮᕤ ᐦᕤᕐᒻᒥᒻ ᐃᒄᒃᓄᕮᕮᒃ ᐸᕐᕰᖑᖤᑐᖓ.
ᐃᓐᖁᕮᒄᒫ, ᐃᒃᕐᖁᒃᕮᒻᒄᒄᒄ ᓄᖓ, ᐸᐸᒃᕮᓄᕐᓄᒄᒄ ᒃᐸᒃᕤᓄᒃ
ᕮᑕᒃᕮᕮᕮᒃᒻᕤᔪᒻ. ᓇᐅᕮᓄ ᕮᔴᕮᒄᒄᔾᒄᖓᒃ ᔪᒻᒫᔪᒃᕮᒄᒃᕮᕮᒄᒃᖓᒃ.
ᒃᕮᕮᒻᓄᒄᒄᒥ, ᑕᕰᕮᓕᒄᒄᒥᖓᒃᖔᖑ ᒃᕰᕮᕮᒻᔴ ᓄᑕᕮᒃᔪᒃᕤᒃᒻᔪᒻᒄᕮᖓ.
ᑕᕮᒪᕤᒄᒄ ᕮᓐᕮᒄᒻᖓᒄ ᑲᕰᒄᕮᒄᒻᒄᕮᓄᒄᕮᒃᖔᕮ ᔪᒄᕮᖔᒄᕮᒄᒄᖓᒄ. ᕮᕮᒃᕮᒄᓇᕰᖓᖓᒃᖓᕮᒄᕮᖓ.
ᐃᓄᕮᒃ ᐅᒃᒃᐸᕮᕮᒻᔪᒄᔪᒻᒄ ᓇᐅᕮᔴᕮᒃᔪᒃᒄᕤ ᐃᓕᔪᕮᒃᔴᕮᕤᕮᒄᒥᕤᒻ,
ᕮᒄᒄᔾᒄ ᔪᕮᒄᒻᒥᒄ ᕮᒄᕮᕰᒻᒣᖤᒻ.

An extract from "The Monster Gull" folklore story
Inuit language has five variations, and a wonderful alphabet, as seen here.

The people

An indigenous person from Nunavut is known as a *Nunavummiut*. While mainstream history claimed Christopher Columbus discovered the Americas, it was more than likely that the hardy Norse explorers were the first "Westerners" to visit these lands. Nunavut itself was probably the land of Helluland, mentioned in the Icelandic epic *The Saga of Erik the Red*.

BEAR SAYS

A good explorer always listens to the local knowledge. It carries the weight of history and experience. Ignore it at your peril!

Bears

When making landfall for camp, we were constantly aware that this was home to wild bears. We expected the most immediate threat to come from polar bears. These magnificent creatures are powerful swimmers, covering great distances between ice floes as they hunt fish. Even their Latin name, *Ursus maritimus*, means "bear of the sea."

BEAR SAYS

Adult polar bears can weigh up to 1,500 pounds and reach 10 feet in length from snout to tail.

Polar bears are the Arctic's apex predators.

Close encounters

Woe betide anyone encountering a mother bear with a newly born cub—that's when these animals are at their most aggressive, to protect their young. I once encountered a huge, lone grizzly bear. At 800 pounds, grizzlies are no less a threat than their polar cousins.

Wild animals

One evening, when we had just pitched camp, we spotted a hungry polar bear nearby. In situations like that, a shotgun and a can of bear spray are vital deterrents—you must protect yourself.

This massive footprint was from a huge bear that we frightened away as we came ashore to camp.

Rescue!

The six of us were alone in this barren wilderness, far from civilization or any other human contact ... or so we thought. To our surprise, we received an emergency satellite phone call from out in the rolling ocean. A fellow adventurer was in trouble near some pack ice. We responded immediately and deviated northward in search of him.

Speeding to the rescue
There is no time to spare when the distress signal comes in!

Inukshuk in Gjoa Haven, Nunavut.

Hitching a lift

We located Mathieu Bonnier, a French adventurer, close to the pack ice at Gjoa Haven, 10 miles from our position. He was attempting to row a small rowing boat across the Northwest Passage, just he and his dog. The wind had blown him toward the pack ice where he would have been dashed to pieces. It took several hours for us to tow him away from the danger zone, but once clear he was able to continue.

The unforgiving wilderness

If we hadn't been passing by, then who would have responded to the call? Once again, it reminded me of Sir John and his poor crew, stranded without any hope of rescue. It demonstrated that, no matter how well prepared you are for an expedition, and no matter how much experience you have, things can and do go wrong. The wilderness is unforgiving.

If we felt vulnerable out in the harsh Arctic Ocean in our boat, I can't imagine how it must have felt for Mathieu in his tiny rowing boat.

The final sprint

Our final leg took us through the 100-mile Dease Strait, between the Kent Peninsula and Victoria Island. We were racing toward our end point—but the weather was turning fast. Angry waves smashed into our RIB and slowed progress. We made camp at Pearce Point for the final night, before pushing on into the Beaufort Sea. True to its name, we were struck by fierce winds.

Tuktoyaktuk
The Hamlet of Tuktoyaktuk was our final destination.

Tuktoyaktuk

The sight of our final destination, the port in Tuktoyaktuk (which translates as "resembling a caribou,") was enough to rally all our battered spirits. Despite the challenges, we had made it in one piece—one of the first RIB boats ever to make the perilous crossing. It was a proud moment for us all.

Adventure's true nature

While we were ecstatic to have crossed uncharted waters with only a few cuts and bruises to show for it, it was sobering to remember how many had perished attempting the same voyage in years gone by. Stumbling across potential members of the Franklin expedition really hit home for me. It was a reminder that all expeditions can be fatal as well as thrilling.

Global warming

Only because of terrible global warming were we able to cross this treacherous route. We had achieved our goal of raising awareness of this critical issue, but I can only hope for the sake of future generations that the passage once again becomes unnavigable, sealing up its secrets as the planet's temperatures settle back down from their current dangerously high levels.

A statue in Hobart, Australia, commemorating Sir John Franklin, whose expedition wintered on Beechey Island in 1846, before sailing on to disaster.

BEAR SAYS

It's a privilege to be able to take part in adventure in this day and age—but it all serves as a reminder that the planet we live on should not be taken for granted.

The frozen sea
This is how the Arctic Ocean should look—before global damage melts it permanently away.

Amundsen and Scott

The unknown southern land

Race to the South Pole

Antarctica is the coldest continent on Earth, and wind, snow, ice, and cloud make its climate one of the most treacherous in the world. It was the last continent to be discovered and the last to be explored. Even now, no one lives there permanently, although many scientists spend time working there. Early geographers believed that evidence pointed to the existence of an "unknown southern land," but no one went near enough to see it until the late 18th century. Sailors continued to visit the seas around Antarctica through the 19th century, some exploring, others hunting seals. At the end of that century, the first land-based explorations were made, and what became known as the "Heroic Age" of Antarctic exploration began, with countries and explorers competing to make new discoveries.

Future rivals

In 1911, Norwegian explorer Roald Amundsen and British explorer Robert Falcon Scott would make two of the greatest Antarctic treks, racing each other to the South Pole.

Roald Amundsen

Robert Falcon Scott

Almost all (98 percent) of Antarctica is covered by ice, much of it more than 1.5 miles thick. In the winter, the sea freezes, forming pack ice— huge pieces of floating ice that cover the water.

First sightings

In 1772–75, James Cook sailed the seas around Antarctica, but saw no land. In 1819, Russian explorer Thaddeus von Bellingshausen spent two years sailing around the continent, and in the next 25 years France, Britain, and the US all sent out expeditions. By 1900 however, only a tiny bit of the land had been explored.

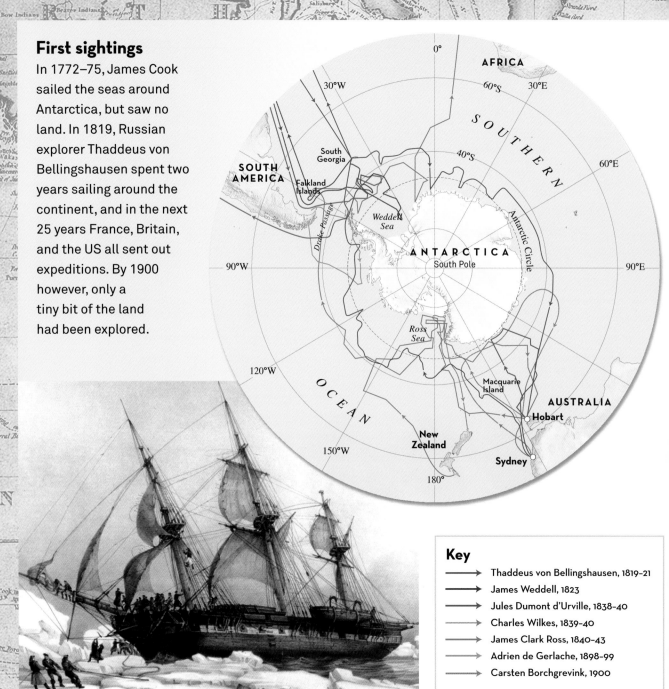

French explorer Jules Dumont d'Urville's fleet skirted the coast of Antarctica in 1838–40. Wooden ships like these could easily be crushed by pack ice.

Key

→ Thaddeus von Bellingshausen, 1819–21
→ James Weddell, 1823
→ Jules Dumont d'Urville, 1838–40
→ Charles Wilkes, 1839–40
→ James Clark Ross, 1840–43
→ Adrien de Gerlache, 1898–99
→ Carsten Borchgrevink, 1900

Scott blazes a trail

The first major land exploration was carried out by the British National Antarctic Expedition of 1901–04, led by Robert Scott. At the Bay of Whales, Scott went up in a tethered hydrogen balloon so that he could look into the interior. From Ross Island, the expedition made two trips by dogsled, going farther inland than anyone had done before.

North
America

Europe

Australia

Antarctica

BEAR SAYS

Virtually uninhabited, Antarctica is the fifth-largest continent: smaller than Asia, Africa, North America, and South America, but larger than Europe and Australia.

Amundsen's first visit

In 1897 Belgian Adrien de Gerlache led an expedition to Antarctica aboard the *Belgica*. Roald Amundsen was one of the crew. In March 1898, the ship was trapped by pack ice. The men developed scurvy, and found the isolation and darkness almost unbearable. It was more than a year before they escaped.

Eyes on the prize

By the beginning of the 20th century, the main goal for Antarctic explorers was to reach the South Pole. Ernest Shackleton had been with Scott in 1902, but the two men had quarreled and Shackleton decided he would get to the pole first. By 1907 he had managed to raise money to equip an old sailing ship, the *Nimrod*, and return to Antarctica. Although he got farther than

Scott had, he decided to turn back about 100 miles from the pole rather than risk the lives of his men. Determined to beat his rival, Scott organized another expedition, sailing on the *Terra Nova*, and reached Antarctica in January 1911. Just as he arrived, Amundsen decided that he too, would try to reach the pole.

Shackleton's team reached their farthest point south on January 9, 1909. They hoisted a British flag before turning back.

BEAR SAYS

Shackleton and his men took a prefabricated hut with them, which they erected at Cape Royds on Ross Island. The hut still stands and is visited regularly by tourists.

National pride

Several other national expeditions were taking place at the time, including the Scottish National Antarctic Expedition of 1902–04.

As well as blazing a trail toward the pole, Shackleton's expedition climbed Mount Erebus and reached the South Magnetic Pole.

Key

→ Discovery Expedition, 1902–03

→ Nimrod Expedition, 1908–09

The race is on

In 1910, Amundsen set off in his ship the *Fram*, saying he was going to explore the North Pole. But once at sea, he changed course and headed south. Soon after, he sent a message to Scott to say that he was on his way. Scott knew what that meant: Amundsen was trying to beat him to the pole. The race had begun!

Heavy weather

To prepare for his assault on the South Pole, Scott gave himself only nine months—most polar explorers took two years—and he spent little time on research and training. The equipment he took along was heavy, which in turn slowed the *Terra Nova*. After leaving New Zealand the ship hit a dreadful storm, and then became trapped in pack ice for three weeks. At last, on January 4, 1911, Scott and his men landed at Cape Evans on Ross Island.

Earlier, Amundsen and his men had spent six months with the Inuits in northern Canada, learning Arctic survival skills, an experience that would prove invaluable.

The long wait

Amundsen and his men reached Antarctica on January 14, 1911, and set up their base at the Bay of Whales. Both the British and Norwegian expeditions then rushed to stock depot camps along their chosen routes to the pole before the start of winter in March. Amundsen's party approached the task in a highly organized way, placing markers to help them find the depots later.

The Norwegians were good skiers and completed the job quickly. In contrast, Scott's men struggled. The sea ice had melted, making it difficult to get from Ross Island to the mainland, and their ponies sank in the snow. They placed few markers and built their main depot farther away from the pole than they had originally planned.

Setting up home

Amundsen's base camp, Framheim, was located on pack ice at the Bay of Whales. There was a risk that the ice might break away and float out to sea, but this site was 62 miles closer to the South Pole than Ross Island.

At the edge of the Ross Ice Shelf in winter (March–September), long hours of darkness are broken only by spells of twilight.

Winter routines

Scott's party built its base at Cape Evans, where it still stands. During the winter, both expeditions worked on repairing and adapting equipment and making everything ready for the trip south. Both parties had plenty of food, but Amundsen wisely had his men eat fresh seal meat every day, which provided lots of vitamin C.

Animal matters

Amundsen had learned from the Inuit how to drive dogsleds, and he took approximately 50 Greenland husky dogs to haul his sleds. Scott brought some dogs but also ponies, which he believed could carry heavier loads. However, the dogs could eat seals and penguins, whereas food for the ponies had to be brought from England.

The worst journey in the world

In midwinter, three of Scott's men set off in the dark for the other side of Ross Island, hoping to find emperor penguin eggs. The temperature fell to -65°F, and the sled they pulled weighed 750 pounds. After five weeks of hardship, they returned, exhausted, but with three eggs. One of the men, Apsley Cherry-Garrard, later recounted the trip in a book called *The Worst Journey in the World*.

Two ways to the pole

Scott planned to follow Shackleton's route toward the pole, via the Beardmore Glacier. Amundsen's route over the Axel Heiberg Glacier meant a shorter journey but was untried and therefore riskier.

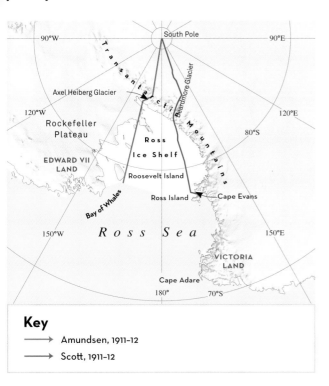

Key

→ Amundsen, 1911–12

→ Scott, 1911–12

First to the Pole

Amundsen and his party set out for the pole on September 8, 1911, but soon returned because of the severe cold. They started again on October 19 and made good progress. Scott and his men left on November 1, but were hampered by their inability to ski well, their inexperience with sled dogs, the difficulties the ponies had walking on the snow, and the breakdown of their motor sleds. Amundsen's men skied 15–20 miles a day, whereas Scott's men managed only about 12 miles. Battling through icy blizzards, Amundsen and the Norwegians moved farther and farther ahead, and reached the South Pole on December 19.

BEAR SAYS

During his time with the Inuit, Amundsen had learned the advantages of wearing several layers of reindeer fur. Air trapped between the layers helped to insulate the wearer.

To ski or not to ski

Skis are faster than snowshoes, and because they spread weight, make it possible to cross thin ice. Coming from Norway, Amundsen and his men had skied all their lives. By contrast, Scott and his men were beginners at skiing, and their equipment was old-fashioned.

A swift ascent

A major challenge for both parties was ascending the Transantarctic Mountains via vast glaciers. On November 17, Amundsen's party reached the foot of the steep Axel Heiberg Glacier. Despite hauling 2,000 pounds of supplies, they and their dogs reached the top in four days, having covered 44 miles and climbed 9,800 feet.

Amundsen

Amundsen took approximately 50 dogs. Some would be killed to feed the other dogs.

Five Norwegians set out and all went to the pole.

Scott

Scott took 33 dogs, but all were sent back from the foot of the Beardmore Glacier.

10 ponies went; all had to be killed before reaching the glacier.

Two motor sleds departed; both soon broke down.

The South Pole conquered

On December 14, after carefully checking their compasses and the distance they had traveled, Amundsen and his men realized they had made it to the South Pole. Holding the post of a Norwegian flag, the men pushed it into the snowy ground and took photographs. The race was won! Although they did not know it, Scott was still 360 miles behind them.

Battling up the Beardmore

Scott and his men chose to drag their sleds up the Beardmore Glacier to the summit 9,800 feet above. Each man was pulling 200 pounds, the snow was soft, and the men frequently sank up to their knees in it. It took them more than three weeks to reach the top of the glacier.

Sixteen Britons set out; eight would go beyond the glacier, five to the pole.

Triumph and tragedy

Scott originally planned to take three men with him to the pole, but changed his mind and took four: Henry Bowers, Edgar Evans, Lawrence Oates, and Edward Wilson. This proved to be a mistake: the tent was too small for five men, extra food was required, and cooking more food took longer. Hauling one sled bearing all their equipment, they struggled on. On January 16, they saw signs of Amundsen's party; a day later, they reached the pole and found the Norwegian flag. Demoralized, they turned homeward, but severe weather set in and all five men perished.

The somber expressions on the faces of Scott and his men tell their story: they had made it to the South Pole, but only after their rivals the Norwegians.

Amundsen

Amundsen and his party set off almost two weeks before the British team. By the time Scott's expedition got underway, Amundsen was already more than 100 miles ahead.

On their return journey, Amundsen and his men enjoyed good weather and found the trip easy going. They arrived back at Framheim on January 29, 1912, with two sleds and 11 dogs, all fit and healthy. A few days later, they sailed for New Zealand.

Scott

By the time Scott's party reached the South Pole, Amundsen and his men were already back on the Ross Ice Shelf. Turning for home, Scott realized he and his men faced a desperate struggle.

Meanwhile, while Scott's team was on its way back, six of his other men were marooned at Cape Adare, 300 miles north of Ross Island. After a terrible winter in an ice cave, they made it back to base camp but left much of their equipment behind.

BEAR SAYS

The average temperature at the South Pole is -56°F, and can be much lower as a result of wind chill. On the return trip, Scott's party experienced intense cold and blizzards.

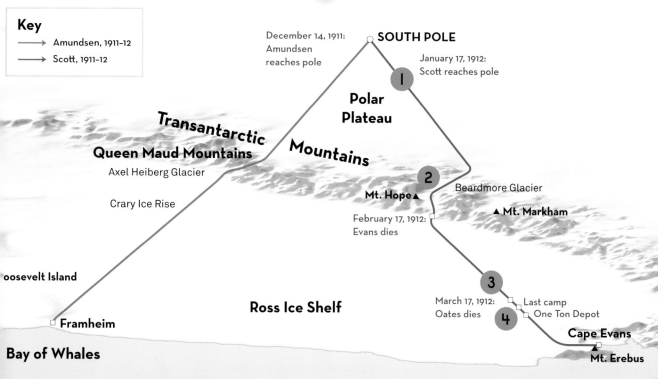

Key

→ Amundsen, 1911–12

→ Scott, 1911–12

December 14, 1911: Amundsen reaches pole

SOUTH POLE

January 17, 1912: Scott reaches pole

1

Polar Plateau

Transantarctic Mountains

Queen Maud Mountains

Axel Heiberg Glacier

Crary Ice Rise

2

Mt. Hope▲

Beardmore Glacier

▲ Mt. Markham

February 17, 1912: Evans dies

Roosevelt Island

Ross Ice Shelf

3

March 17, 1912: Oates dies

Last camp

One Ton Depot

4

□ Framheim

Cape Evans

Bay of Whales

Mt. Erebus

ROSS SEA

Noble, but exhausting

Scott believed that "man hauling" the sleds to the pole was nobler than using dogs. But dragging the heavy loads drained the strength of his men.

Heavy going

On their way back, Scott and his men spent a day collecting rock samples on the Beardmore Glacier. These added over 31 pounds to the sleds, delaying the party further.

3

Oates walks out

By mid-March, Oates was in constant pain from frostbite and ill from lack of food. Aware that he was hampering progress, on the morning of March 17, he walked out of the tent into a blizzard. He was never seen again.

4

Last words

Scott's last diary entry was dated March 29, 1912. Scott, Bowers, and Wilson died of cold and starvation, only 11 miles from the next food store, One Ton Depot. A search party found their bodies on November 12.

Antarctica unveiled

Amundsen's achievement was celebrated around the world. Despite his failure, Scott was hailed as a hero in his day, but later historians criticized his poor decision-making. By the end of the Heroic Age of Exploration in 1917, less than five percent of Antarctica had been mapped. Since World War II, however, the use of aerial photography and satellite technology, as well as further pioneering treks by explorers, including Ann Bancroft, Børge Ousland, and Phillip Law, have greatly expanded our knowledge of Antarctica. In the late 1950s, the international community took steps to protect the continent from territorial claims and exploitation, and preserve it for peaceful purposes. Today, it is visited not only by scientists, but also by increasing numbers of tourists.

The South Pole is now the site of the Amundsen-Scott South Pole Station. The location of the pole is marked with a plaque, which has to be repositioned each year to compensate for the movement of the polar ice sheet, which shifts about an inch a day.

BEAR SAYS

Anarctica has no government of its own, but seven countries claim slices of the continent: Argentina, Australia, Chile, France, New Zealand, Norway, and the United Kingdom.

ANTARCTIC MILESTONES			
1928	**1946–47**	**1957–58**	**1991**
Australian Sir Hubert Wilkins makes the first airplane flight over Antarctica.	Operation Highjump, run by the US Navy, becomes the largest Antarctic expedition ever mounted. More than 70,000 aerial photographs are taken.	Major nations take part in the International Geophysical Year, collaborating on research projects. This leads to the Antarctic Treaty of 1959, which bans military activity and preserves the continent for scientific research.	The Madrid Protocol forbids mining and mineral exploitation in Antarctica for the next 50 years and places strict environmental restrictions on tourism.

Later heroes

The Heroic Age continued until the outbreak of World War I. One of the most remarkable later expeditions was the Australasian Antarctic Expedition of 1911–14, led by Douglas Mawson, which mapped large areas of the coast. On one outing, one of Mawson's two companions fell into a crevasse, along with most of their dogs and supplies. Soon after, his remaining companion died and he had to march 99 miles back to base alone.

In 1913, a large cross was erected on Observation Hill, near where Scott and his men died. It was inscribed with their names and the words "To strive, to seek, to find, and not to yield." This spirit of adventure lives on today in the work of the many scientists and explorers still investigating the wonders of this remote land.

Antarctic tourism began in the 1950s and has increased rapidly in the last 30 years. A visit to Antarctica is the trip of a lifetime for many people, but the ever-growing number of visitors also represents a significant threat to Antarctica's fragile environment.

Amundsen's final journey

Amundsen continued to explore the polar regions. But, in 1928, his plane crashed in the Arctic and he disappeared without a trace.

Reference
How explorers navigated

Navigation is the art of working out where you are and where you want to go by means of astronomy, mathematics, and/or specialized instruments. In the early days of exploration, sailors and other travelers used the position of the sun, the planets, and the stars to guide them, especially when sailing out of sight of land where there were no fixed reference points. Later, tools were invented that helped travelers navigate more accurately. A compass indicated which way was north. By comparing the direction of travel according to the compass to a compass drawn on a map, a traveler could plot their direction from place to place. A telescope allowed sailors and explorers to see landmarks from a great distance.

To plot position more accurately however, explorers needed to determine their latitude and longitude. Latitude describes how far north or south you are, relative to the Equator. Longitude describes your position east or west of the Greenwich Meridian, also known as the Prime Meridian or International Meridian, an imaginary line passing through the Royal Greenwich Observatory in London, England. Both are measured in degrees, and together they can pinpoint any location on Earth.

To determine their latitude, explorers measured the height of the sun at noon and then consulted printed tables that noted where the sun would be at noon at different latitudes and at different times of the year. Instruments for measuring the height of the sun (relative to the instrument) included the astrolabe and the quadrant. These were however, difficult to use accurately, especially in bad weather.

To work out longitude required more precise measurements, and therefore more sophisticated instruments. The most widely used was the sextant, which appeared in the 18th century. This device incorporates two mirrors, a small telescope, and a sliding measuring scale. The user looks through the telescope at the horizon and moves the mirrors until the reflection of the sun, moon, or a particular star lines up with the horizon. The angle between the horizon and the sun, moon, or star can then be read off the measuring scale, and along with the precise time of day, checked against printed tables to obtain both the latitude and longitude.

HISTORICAL TIMELINE

1776	US Declaration of Independence
1788	First British colony established in Australia
1789	French Revolution
1795	Britain takes over Cape Colony in southern Africa
1804–06	Lewis and Clark expedition
1815	Napoleon defeated at Battle of Waterloo
1825	First passenger-carrying railroad built in England
1833	Slavery abolished in the British Empire
1836	Dutch "Boer" settlers found Orange Free State in southern Africa
1838	First commercial use of electric telegraph
1841	Livingstone arrives in Africa
1848	US annexes California and New Mexico
1849	Start of Gold Rush in California
1853	Crimean War begins
1856	Livingstone returns to Britain
1858	Livingstone begins Zambezi Expedition
1860	Burke and Wills expedition sets off
1861	US Civil War begins; Burke and Wills die
1863	Livingstone returns to Britain
1865	US Civil War ends; slavery is abolished in the US
1866	Livingstone returns to Africa to search for source of Nile
1869	First transcontinental railroad completed in the US; Suez Canal opens
1870	Franco-Prussian War begins
1871	Stanley travels to Africa and finds Livingstone
1873	Death of Livingstone in Africa
1876	Alexander Graham Bell invents telephone
1877	Stanley completes Trans-Africa Expedition
1879	Thomas Edison invents electric light
1886	Stanley starts expedition to relieve Emin Pasha
1889	First car manufacturer founded in France
1896	Italian Guglielmo Marconi patents first wireless telegraphs, in London
1899–1902	Boer War in South Africa between Britain and Boer settlers
1901	Australia becomes independent nation
1902–1903	Scott makes first overland journeys in Antarctica
1903	Orville and Wilbur Wright make first powered flight, in US
1906	San Francisco earthquake; Amundsen locates North Magnetic Pole

Although the Global Positioning System (GPS), which uses satellites to pinpoint the user's location, has replaced sextants for day-to-day navigation, many modern sailors still take a sextant with them when they go to sea because it is not dependent on electricity or satellite technology, and therefore makes a reliable backup tool.

Cartography, the drawing of maps or charts, advanced alongside the development of navigational instruments. The maps drawn by explorers, such as those by Lewis and Clark, made an important contribution to later travelers' ability to find their way through the wilderness or across the oceans.

Glossary

Arid—Very dry, or receiving little or no rain.

Cache—A hidden store of supplies. Explorers often buried or concealed caches of equipment for use on their return along the same route.

Crevasse—A deep, open crack in a glacier or ice field. If covered with snow, a crevasse can be difficult to detect.

Dehydration—Excessive loss of water from the body, usually as a result of heat and/or intense exercise.

Depot—A place for storing supplies.

Dormant—Temporarily inactive. A dormant plant is alive but not growing; a dormant animal is in a form of sleep.

Dysentery—A disease that causes severe diarrhea.

Inuit—The native people of northern Canada and parts of Greenland and Alaska.

Keelboat—A flat-bottomed riverboat.

Mangrove—A type of tree or shrub that grows in muddy swamps. Its tangled roots often stick out above the ground.

Missionary—A person who goes to another country to try to spread a religious faith.

Monsoon season—The wet season in northern Australia, southern Asia, and central-western Africa, which brings strong winds and heavy rainfall.

Pass—A gap or low area in a range of mountains where it is possible to cross the range.

Portage—To carry a boat and its cargo overland from one waterway to another.

Rift valley—A valley with steep sides, formed when land between two fractures in Earth's crust drops downward.

Scurvy—An illness caused by a lack of vitamin C, which leads to bleeding under the skin, bleeding gums, and extreme weakness. Vitamin C is found in fresh fruit and vegetables, and also in seal meat.

Source—The place where a river starts flowing, usually a spring.

Stockade—An enclosure built using upright wooden posts or stakes.

Tectonic plate—A large segment of the Earth's crust. Tectonic plates move constantly, though very slowly.

Terrain—An area of land, or the form of an area of land.

Transcontinental—Extending across a continent or continents.

Picture credits

Index